TWAYNE'S WORLD AUTHORS SERIES

A Survey of the World's Literature

Sylvia E. Bowman, Indiana University

GENERAL EDITOR

CANADA

Joseph Jones, University of Texas

EDITOR

Morley Callaghan

(TWAS 1)

TWAYNE'S WORLD AUTHORS SERIES (TWAS)

The purpose of TWAS is to survey the major writers —novelists, dramatists, historians, poets, philosophers, and critics—of the nations of the world. Among the national literatures covered are those of Australia, Canada, China, Eastern Europe, France, Germany, Greece, India, Italy, Japan, Latin America, New Zealand, Poland, Russia, Scandinavia, Spain, and the African nations, as well as Hebrew, Yiddish, and Latin Classical literatures. This survey is complemented by Twayne's United States Authors Series and English Authors Series.

The intent of each volume in these series is to present a critical-analytical study of the works of the writer; to include biographical and historical material that may be necessary for understanding, appreciation, and critical appraisal of the writer; and to present all material in clear, concise English—but not to vitiate the scholarly content of the work by doing so.

Morley Callaghan

By BRANDON CONRON

University of Western Ontario

Twayne Publishers, Inc. :: New York

To Caroline

Preface

More than twenty years ago in wartime London, William Saroyan is reported to have asked a Canadian correspondent, "What ever happened to Morley Callaghan?" It was at that time a pertinent question. After a spectacularly successful start, after being praised by the most distinguished authors of the day, his stories in all the leading magazines, six full-length novels and two collections of stories published by 1937, Callaghan seemed to have lost creative energy and to have faded into literary obscurity.

For nearly ten years he wrote only articles and reviews. By regular participation in panels for the Canadian Broadcasting Corporation he became better known in his own country as a controversial radio personality than as an author. Turning again to fiction in the late forties, Callaghan began another period of prolific creative output. The novels and the autobiographical reminiscences of this later period are evidence of his continuing artistic power.

From his first publication he was recognized almost unanimously by the critics as a masterful short story writer. Although his early novels, too, were favorably reviewed, the critical reception given his post-war work was mixed. As recently as 1960 Edmund Wilson in *The New Yorker* called him "perhaps the most unjustly neglected novelist in the English speaking world." Happily since then, however, the originality and vitality of Callaghan's fictional presentation have been increasingly recognized. Several of his novels have been translated into various European languages. New editions of early books and reprints of later ones in both hard and soft covers are coming out in North America and England. His stories are included in anthologies around the world. A pirated version of *More Joy in Heaven* even appeared in a Russian magazine in 1962. His youthful association on terms of familiar equality with such famous figures as Sinclair Lewis,

James Joyce, Ernest Hemingway and Scott Fitzgerald, as recalled in *That Summer in Paris,* has aroused a new interest in Callaghan's career.

In his person and writings he is emerging not only as a literary link between the revolt against sham of the post-World War I decade and the revolt against sentimentality of the post-World War II era, but also as a writer whose themes and characters reflect in a haunting and memorable way the central concerns of contemporary life. Beneath the surface of his absorbing fictional action is a complex and compassionate exploration of man's mind and heart. Looking steadily at life without any shallow optimism, Callaghan suggests that the aware individual who examines himself with honesty, and his fellow humans with unlimited tolerance, can find a satisfactory solution to the clash between spiritual and empirical values. The secret of the good life—a happy acceptance and reconciliation of both flesh and spirit—is the same for enlightened modern man as it was for Socrates. Like the latter, in ironically probing various aspects of society's conventions and mores, Callaghan is a natural iconoclast of prejudice, injustice and lingering taboos. Unlike some of his older American contemporaries, he has steadfastly refused to withdraw from active involvement in life or to allow himself to be surrounded by an aura of myth or legend. Frequent appearances on radio and television in Canada have interrupted his work as a writer and undoubtedly taken luster from the reading public's romantic image of an artist's splendid isolation. Yet this activity has also kept him in touch with contemporary issues and living idiom.

Canada's finest novelist at sixty-two is a genial and unassuming extrovert who can look back on forty years of writing with the satisfaction of knowing that he has never prostituted his art: the fact that his fiction on occasion has been the object of library bans and adverse criticism has not deflected his artistic integrity. As his seventeenth book nears completion, moreover, his unfailing confidence in the quality of his work seems likely to be justified. Posterity may well accord him the right to employ Fielding's observation, "I am myself a better judge than any pitiful critic."

This first comprehensive published study of Callaghan's career provides for readers unfamiliar with the large body of his work what might be described as criticism by exposition. To illuminate the critical analysis there are included biographical details drawn not only from already published sources but also from material gathered in conversations with Callaghan himself.

This volume has been completed with the generous cooperation of Morley Callaghan and his wife Loretto. I should also like to acknowledge Mr. Callaghan's kind permission to quote from those books to which he holds personal copyright.

In addition I wish to express gratitude to the following publishers for permission to quote from the books and articles listed:

Coward-McCann Inc., for permission to quote from Morley Callaghan, *The Many Colored Coat* (1960), *A Passion in Rome* (1961), and *That Summer in Paris* (1963).

Macmillan Co. of New York, for permission to quote from Morley Callaghan, *The Loved and The Lost* (1951).

Macmillan Co. of Canada, for permission to quote from Morley Callaghan, *The Loved and The Lost* (1951), *Morley Callaghan's Stories* (1959), *The Many Colored Coat* (1960), *A Passion in Rome* (1961), and *That Summer in Paris* (1963).

McClelland and Stewart Ltd., for permission to quote from the Introductions to the following "New Canadian Library" editions of Morley Callaghan: *Such Is My Beloved* (Malcolm Ross), *They Shall Inherit The Earth* (Frank W. Watt), and *More Joy in Heaven* (Hugo McPherson).

Queens Quarterly, for permission to quote from Hugo McPherson, "The Two Worlds of Morley Callaghan" (LXIV, 3, Autumn, 1957).

Royal Society of Canada, for permission to quote from Frank R. Scott, "Morley Callaghan" (*Proceedings of the Royal Society of Canada*, 54, 1960).

St. Martin's Press of New York, for permission to quote from Morley Callaghan, *Morley Callaghan's Stories* (1959).

Saturday Night, for permission to quote from Wyndham Lewis, "What Books for Total War?" (LVIII, 5, October 10, 1942).

Charles Scribner's Sons, for permission to quote from *Editor to Author. The Letters of Maxwell E. Perkins* (1950), edited by John Hall Wheelock.

The Canadian Forum, for permission to quote from Margaret Avison, "Callaghan Revisited" (vol. 39, March, 1960).

The New York Times, for permission to quote from R. G. Davis,

"Carla, Sam and a Dying Pope" (Book Review Section, October 15, 1961).

The New Yorker, for permission to quote from Edmund Wilson, "Morley Callaghan of Toronto" (XXXVI, 41, Nov. 26, 1960), and "That Summer in Paris" (XXXIX, 1, Feb. 23, 1963).

The Tamarack Review, for permission to quote from Robert Weaver, "A Talk With Morley Callaghan" (vol. 7, Spring, 1958).

The University of Toronto Press, for permission to quote from Milton Wilson, "Literature in English" (*Canadian Annual Review for 1960,* 1961).

I am indebted to Mr. William R. Poole, Q.C. for locating a copy of *No Man's Meat,* to Mrs. Dora Mavor Moore and Mr. J. Mavor Moore for their assistance in providing material on Callaghan's plays, to my colleagues Carl F. Klinck and Geoffrey Rans, to Miss Sylvia E. Bowman, Professor Joseph Jones and their associates for offering helpful suggestions on the manuscript.

Finally, I wish to thank the University of Western Ontario for a grant-in-aid toward the completion of this book.

BRANDON CONRON

The University of Western Ontario
June, 1965

Contents

Chronology

1903   Edward Morley Callaghan born February 22 in Toronto, Ontario, son of Roman Catholic parents of Irish descent, Thomas and Mary (Dewan) Callaghan.

1909-
1921   Attended Withrow Public School and Riverdale Collegiate, where as a Grade 11 student he sold his first publication, a descriptive piece on Yonge and Albert Streets, Toronto, to the *Star Weekly* for twelve dollars.

1921   Entered St. Michael's College, University of Toronto, and participated in such extramural activities as debating, baseball, hockey and boxing.

1923   Took a summer position on the Toronto *Daily Star* and worked as a reporter for four summers as well as three afternoons a week during subsequent academic years. Associated for several weeks with Ernest Hemingway, then European correspondent for the *Star Weekly*, who encouraged him in his writing.

1924   Met his future wife, Loretto, an art student, at a college dance.

1925   Graduated with a B.A. degree in general arts from St. Michael's College, University of Toronto. Enrolled in Osgoode Hall Law School, Toronto, and articled to a law firm.

1926   First short story to be published, "A Girl With Ambition," appeared in Paris in *This Quarter*. "Last Spring They Came Over" was accepted for an issue of *transition*. Started to write novel *Strange Fugitive*. Visited New York briefly and met such literary figures as Nathan Asch, Ford Madox Ford, Josephine Herbst and her husband John Herrman, Katherine Ann Porter, Allen Tate and William Carlos Williams. Opened the Viking Lending Library in a basement of Richmond Street West, Toronto, along with friend Art Kent.

1927   Short stories appeared in American and European magazines and "Amuck in the Bush" in *The American Caravan* yearbook.

1928   Met Max Perkins of Scribner's Sons, New York, who bought three stories for the July and August issues of *Scribner's Magazine*, and agreed to publish *Strange Fugitive* as well as a book of short stories. Graduated from Osgoode Hall Law School and admitted to the Ontario Bar. Novel, *Strange Fugitive*, published (Scribner's). "A Country Passion," by its publication in J. Edward O'Brien's *Best Short Stories*, marked the beginning of Callaghan's continuous inclusion for fourteen years in that annual edition.

1929   Collection of short stories, *A Native Argosy*, published (Scribner's). Married Loretto Florence Dee, daughter of Joseph and Catherine (Hamlin) Dee, April 16, in Toronto. Travelled via New York to Paris. Remained until late autumn in Paris, associating with Hemingway, Fitzgerald, Joyce, writer-publisher Robert McAlmon of Contact Press and Edward Titus, editor of *This Quarter*. Completed novel *It's Never Over* and novella *No Man's Meat*. Wrote stories for such magazines as *Atlantic Monthly, Esquire, Harper's Bazaar, Scribner's* and *The New Yorker*. Returned home to Toronto via London and Dublin.

1930   Novel, *It's Never Over*, published (Scribner's). Lived for eight months between an old farm house in Pennsylvania and a hotel in New York City, writing stories for leading American magazines before returning to Toronto to take up permanent residence.

1931   Novella of 42 pages, *No Man's Meat*, published in Paris in limited autographed edition by E. W. Titus.

1932   Novel, *A Broken Journey*, published (Scribner's).
A son, Michael Burke, born November 20.

1934   Novel, *Such Is My Beloved*, published (Scribner's).

1935   Novel, *They Shall Inherit The Earth*, published (Macmillan).

1936 *Now That April's Here and Other Stories,* published (Random House).
      Lived in New York for six months.
1937 Novel, *More Joy in Heaven,* published (Random House).
      A son, Barry Morley Joseph, born July 5.
1939 Unpublished plays, *Turn Again Home,* purchased by the New York Theatre Guild and rehearsed for production but not presented, and *Just Ask for George,* written.
1940 Became a regular contributor to *New World Magazine,* to which he submitted monthly commentaries until it was absorbed in 1948 into *National Home Monthly* which subsequently ceased publication.
1942 Went to sea for the summer in a Royal Canadian Navy corvette to do a script for the National Film Board. Began a book with a naval background.
1943 Chairman of a Canadian Broadcasting Corporation radio program first called "Things to Come" and later known as "Citizen's Forum," with which he travelled across Canada until 1947.
1946 Older brother, Burke, died at the age of 44.
1947 Participated in new CBC radio quiz show, "Beat the Champs," and started turning out short stories again.
1948 Began writing *The Loved and The Lost.*
      Juvenile novel, *Luke Baldwin's Vow,* an expansion of a *Saturday Evening Post* story, published (Winston).
      Fictionalized description of the University of Toronto, *The Varsity Story,* published (Macmillan).
      Father died, December 6, at the age of 76.
1949 Unpublished play, *To Tell the Truth,* originally called *Just Ask for George* (1939), performed in spring season by the New Play Society at the Museum Theatre Stage, and later moved to the Royal Alexandra Theatre, Toronto.
1950 Unpublished play, *Going Home,* originally called *Turn Again Home* (1939), performed by the New Play Society at the Museum Theatre Stage, Toronto. Launched CBC radio show, "Now I Ask You," and became a regular guest on a television program, "Fighting Words."
      Mother died, December 28, at the age of 80.

1951 Novel, *The Loved and The Lost,* published (Macmillan). Won the Governor General's Award for fiction in 1951.

1955 Novella, *The Man With The Coat,* published in *Maclean's Magazine,* won its $5,000.00 novel award.

1958 Spent a few weeks in Rome on a journalistic assignment at the time of Pope Pius XII's death, and began to write *A Passion in Rome.*

1959 Selection of his favorite stories, *Morley Callaghan's Stories,* published (Macmillan).

1960 Novel, *The Many Colored Coat,* which grew out of *The Man With The Coat,* published (Coward-McCann).

1961 Novel, *A Passion in Rome,* published (Coward-McCann).

1963 Autobiographical reminiscence, *That Summer in Paris,* recounting his association in Paris in 1929 with such famous literary figures as Hemingway, Fitzgerald and Joyce, published (Coward-McCann). Began working on a novel, *Thumbs Down on Julien Jones,* with a wartime setting first in New York and then at sea.

1965 Awarded an honorary Doctor of Letters degree by the University of Western Ontario.

Morley Callaghan

CHAPTER 1

This Happy Acceptance of Reality

FROM his early years Callaghan had been encouraged in an enjoyment of literature by a congenial home atmosphere of books, music and politics. During his late teens he became an enthusiastic reader of modern American fiction. Even before he entered college he had begun turning his own experiences into stories that were characterized by a sharpness and clarity of language. His work as a reporter for the Toronto *Daily Star* during several summers developed a youthful interest in writing, provided fresh ideas for stories, and gave him the opportunity to meet Hemingway. By the time he had graduated in arts and law Callaghan had attracted literary attention with the appearance of his short stories in European and American magazines and with the publication of his first novel. All of these writings are characterized by an attitude which he describes as a "happy acceptance of reality" and by the stylistic aim "to tell the truth cleanly."

I *Celtic-Canadian Heritage*

Edward Morley Callaghan was born in Toronto on February 22, 1903, the younger son of Roman Catholic parents of Irish descent. The family surname, although pronounced Cállahan of recent years, was originally Cállagan. His father, Thomas, who was born in Wales and came to Canada as a youth, became a dispatcher with the Canadian National Railway Express. His mother, Mary Dewan, was born in Collingwood on Georgian Bay. This Ontario town, where as a boy, Callaghan spent summer holidays with his aunt, is the setting for many of his later writings.

Each side of the family brought a heritage of literary and political interest. Thomas Callaghan regularly contributed satirical verse to the *Telegram* and to *The Moon*, a comic journal published for several years around the turn of the century. Both parents read poetry to their boys (Poe was a favourite author), and encouraged the singing talent of their older son, Burke. They were both active in Liberal clubs. A keen debater and ardent political worker, Thomas named his first son after Edmund Burke, the champion of free trade with Ireland and of Catholic Emancipation, and his second son after John Morley, biographer of Burke and twice chief secretary for Ireland in the Liberal government of William Gladstone.

In this congenial and lively cultural atmosphere Morley Callaghan's own enjoyment of literature came naturally. He attended Withrow Public School and Riverdale Collegiate, where he displayed an easy academic competence and excelled in athletics. He was pitcher of the baseball team and junior captain of the football team. As a student in Grade Eleven he sold for twelve dollars to the *Star Weekly* his first published work, a descriptive piece on Yonge and Albert Streets, Toronto. Yet it was not until he was eighteen and had nearly finished high school that he became intensely interested in contemporary writing. He began to read in particular the stories of Sherwood Anderson, Ruth Suckow and Somerset Maugham, published in the New York monthly magazine *The Smart Set*.[1] This fiction seemed to have a reality which brought the world very close.

For Callaghan then, as still today, Canada was part of the North-American rather than the European cultural pattern. The historical romances of the colonial era, late nineteenth and early twentieth centuries, had little relevance for the contemporary period. The novels of John Richardson, Charles G. D. Roberts, William Kirby and Gilbert Parker presented images of Canada which Callaghan could not accept. Charles William Gordon's ("Ralph Connor") use of Western settings as a picturesque backdrop for melodramatic evangelism, L. M. Montgomery's girls' series and Mazo de la Roche's early depictions of Jalna's domestic world were too decorous in their limited realism to appeal. Frederick Philip Grove had just begun to publish his sober presentations of prairie pioneer life, but his dour personality, his themes and setting were alien to Callaghan. Of his own countrymen, Raymond Knister alone was attempting to develop, in the rural stories contributed to the *Star Weekly* and to Canadian and American *avant-garde* magazines, an independent style with a realistic sharpness and clarity of expression that Callaghan found congenial. He later enjoyed a short association with Knister, an isolated personality, who included "Last Spring They Came Over" in his anthology of *Canadian Short Stories* (1928).

It was primarily American and European writers, then, who influenced Callaghan's early literary career. By the time he was twenty, as he himself remarks, "I was also reading wildly. I read Dostoevski, Joseph Conrad, Sinclair Lewis, Flaubert; *The Dial*, *The Adelphi*, and the old *Smart Set*, edited by H. L. Mencken and George Jean Nathan; Catherine Mansfield, D. H. Lawrence—everything." [2] But "the popular writers of the day like Hergesheimer, Edith Wharton, James Branch Cabell, Galsworthy, Hugh Walpole, H. G. Wells—except for *Tono Bungay* . . ." [3] he rejected fiercely as more intent on showing off their education than on facing and giving a fresh description of subjects and experience. Instead of their "upholstered" prose, Callaghan preferred the direct, simple language of Sherwood Anderson, who was for him his "literary father."

Callaghan's own experiences became material for fiction. During his high school years his summer employment—travelling over large sections of Ontario by horse and buggy as a magazine salesman, or working as a lumberyard hand for two weeks—and his knowledge of department store life gained by selling neckties in Simpson's during Christmas holidays, provided authentic background for later stories. The summer before he entered the university he wrote three stories about a character called Old Mac who worked in Simpson's Department Store, and sold them to a Toronto magazine known as the *National Pictorial*. But it went bankrupt just before the stories were to be published, and Callaghan was not paid for his efforts.

II *Young Journalist*

Already fired with the ambition to write, and experimenting with a realistic technique, Callaghan took a summer position in 1923 on the Toronto *Daily Star*. His training as a reporter provided him with a fresh source of ideas for short stories on which he worked in his free time. That same summer too, he met Ernest Hemingway, then European correspondent for the *Star*, who had returned to Toronto because of his wife's pregnancy and a desire to provide their unborn child with a stable home during his infancy. Hemingway's *Three Poems and Ten Stories* had recently been printed in Paris, and he expected to have considerable freedom to develop his craft while writing under his own by-line. But he was subjected to the humiliation of petty assignments by the celebrated Harry Comfort Hindmarsh, who had married the publisher's daughter and was then assistant-managing editor.[4] Callaghan became friendly with Hemingway, read his stories and discussed with him writers like Sherwood Anderson, James Joyce, Ezra Pound and Scott Fitzgerald. The first story which Callaghan brought Hemingway, a piece which was never published, was set in the district of Toronto's St. Michael's Cathedral and the nearby Labor Temple. After reading it, Hemingway "said quietly, 'you're a real writer. You write big-time stuff. All you have to do is keep on writing.'"[5] By the time Hemingway returned to Europe at the end of the summer, Callaghan had been encouraged in his own writing and promised to send his best work on to Paris.

After this Toronto association with Hemingway, Callaghan continued to write with great confidence. During the academic year 1923-24, in which he met his future wife Loretto at a college dance, he turned out such stories as "A Girl With Ambition," "Last Spring They Came Over" and "A Wedding Dress." These won critical approval from Hemingway, who eventually passed them on to people like Ford Madox Ford, then editing the *Transatlantic Review* in Paris, Robert McAlmon of Contact Press, and the editors of *transition* and *This Quarter*.

Yet it was two years before any of these pieces was to be published. Meantime, Callaghan, who was working on a short novel, had graduated in 1925 with a B.A. degree from St. Michael's College, University of Toronto, had enrolled in Osgoode Hall Law School and was articled to a local law firm. Still working part-time for the *Star*, he reflected in many stories of this period his experiences as a reporter. In the winter of 1925-26 the first of these stories was published: "A Girl With Ambition" appeared in *This Quarter*, edited by Ernest Walsh in Paris. Within a few months "Last Spring They Came Over" was accepted for a later issue of *transition* (June, 1927). In 1926, along with a friend, Art Kent, Callaghan opened a little bookstore, the Viking Lending Library, in a basement of Richmond Street West, opposite Osgoode Hall.

Although the venture was not a financial success, it did provide "a good hangout" for writing stories during the next two years.

In the autumn of 1926 Callaghan took a trip to New York in order to see friends of Hemingway and McAlmon who could give him news of Paris. On this occasion, and on subsequent visits as a law student, he met Josephine Herbst and her husband John Herrman, novelist Nathan Asch, Katherine Ann Porter, William Carlos Williams, Allan Tate and Ford Madox Ford. Throughout that year letters from McAlmon and Hemingway continued to arrive, and people with Paris connections increasingly visited Callaghan in Toronto in the summer of 1927. Asch spent some time there; Raymond Knister, Canadian poet and short story writer, whose work had also appeared in *This Quarter,* introduced himself. Ezra Pound wrote from Rapallo, Italy, to say that he had accepted two stories, "A Predicament" and "Ancient Lineage," for publication in a single issue of his *Exile.* Max Perkins at Scribner's in New York, after reading "Amuck in the Bush" in *The American Caravan* of 1927 and listening to Scott Fitzgerald's enthusiastic praise of Callaghan's work[6] wanted to see more stories. Accordingly, during the early part of 1928, Callaghan went to New York to meet Max Perkins, who agreed that Scribner's would publish in that year *Strange Fugitive,* some stories (including "A Predicament" released by Pound) in *Scribner's Magazine,* and a book of short stories the following season.

III *Strange Fugitive* (1928)

Although Callaghan had attracted literary attention with his short stories, his first published book was *Strange Fugitive.* Set in Toronto during the Prohibition era, this novel deals with a general theme that is frequently treated by Callaghan: the problem of the individual unable to adjust to society. Harry Trotter, a young lumberyard foreman with a sadistic and bullying streak in his nature, is fired for beating up an Italian employee. Unable to find other work that will satisfy his own self-importance, he turns to bootlegging and leaves his wife for a more exciting divorcée. After a year of successful operation, including hijacking and murder, he is gunned down in the street by a rival gang.

Unlike Scott Fitzgerald's romantic bootlegger, Jay Gatsby, Harry Trotter as a hero is neither glamorous nor imaginative. He is ordinary in the sense of being undistinguished rather than being representative of middle-class morality in Toronto. His presentation reflects the influence of Zola, for his behavior has been conditioned by both heredity and environment. His father, who was a factory cloth-worker, spent all his spare time painting pictures that never quite made the annual Gallery exhibitions; he disregarded the art committee's advice that he should take a few lessons, persisted in going his own unregulated way, and died frustrated. Harry slept with his mother until he was nine, and as a young man felt a kinship with her as he recalled her love of "Fall weather when trees were bare and the winds got cold." [7] Yet despite the naturalistic influence of heredity and environment, his frustrated temperament and Oedipus complex, Harry's career and eventual doom result finally from his own freedom of moral choice.

The novel is divided structurally into four parts and presented in the setting of Canada's largest English-speaking city, Toronto, as it was in the twenties. Already the difficulties of post-war reconstruction are appearing in the growing problem of unemployment, aggravated by the shift of agrarian workers to larger industrialized cities and by the influx of immigrants from Europe. The increased interest in such movements as Communism and Fascism and the general relaxation of puritanical moral standards, as a partial result of the influence of European customs on veterans who had served abroad during the war, are evident. Against this background Harry Trotter is introduced in Part I as a slave-driving gang boss of a lumberyard, affectionately dominating his small, sentimental wife Vera, who sometimes thinks of him "as a man who in other days on barbaric islands would have been a tribal chief." [8] Subordinate to his governing lust for power is his sensual desire for women. Sullen and discontented after losing his job, he quickly turns to a divorcée, Anna, for comfort and seeks an outlet for his restlessness in listening to political addresses at the Labor Temple and planning to go on the road selling magazines with his agreeable college-trained friend, Jimmie Nash.

In Part II Harry's discontent, crystallized by the remarks of a Communist acquaintance, "A young man should live alone. . . . a wife gets in the way of a man's bright ideas," [9] brings him to a night of decision. After leaving Vera, spending some time in a speakeasy and provoking an anti-semitic brawl in a dance-hall, he persuades Nash to help him steal a truck load of booze.

Part III outlines their developing bootlegging career. Nash's ingenuity discovers ways of circumventing the Liquor Act, and Trotter's strength and confidence make the operation a success. Easy money encourages them to live more elaborately and gives Harry a feeling of power. Although often thinking of Vera and increasingly dissatisfied with his life, he becomes more deeply involved in violent crimes in order to maintain and expand his empire. When one of his own men is found murdered, Harry decides to intimidate his enemies by killing his chief rival, Cosantino, in cold blood, and later calmly attends his funeral.

In Part IV, impressed by the tombstones in the cemetery where Cosantino is buried, Harry feels impelled to return to his parents' home-town, Maydale, and erect over their graves imposing granite pillars. Memories of his mother naturally turn his thoughts to his wife Vera, and his happier past. Fed up with his mistress, Anna, depressed and remorseful, he resolves to return to Vera, but before their proposed reunion he is killed in the street by rival gangsters.

The narrative of *Strange Fugitive,* which is replete with violent melodrama, drunken brawls, face-slapping and murder, is presented mainly through the sensuous perceptions and thoughts of the chief figure, Harry Trotter. Character is revealed by actions which are made to appear natural and by dialogue that for the most part keeps in cultural and psychological key with the various individuals. There is an objectivity of treatment which discourages the reader from making any moral judgment, and which made the writing seem "hard-boiled" at the time when the novel was published. Beneath the surface events and conscious thoughts expressed, however, are motivations which soften the impact of this naturalistic approach and heighten interest. Contributing to the suspense is the sense of foreboding experienced by many of the characters, especially throughout the second half of the novel. The skilful description of unpleasant seasonal or weather conditions, of bitter cold or pouring rain at critical moments, underlines the mood of impending disaster. The most typical structural devices employed in this early work are symbolism and irony.

There are two particularly striking symbols which are developed at length. The first is the image of the Catholic cathedral. To the Communist agitator, Isaac Pimblett, it represents "the ultra-respectable class. . . . you can't get away from it. It's right in the centre of things," [10] and the message of its chimes interrupts and obliterates the rantings of materialism. To Harry it is a reminder of Vera (Truth), and even though the cathedral partially burns down, the carillon bells still ring from its tower just as "the old thoughts of Vera he had been trying to avoid" [11] come back continually to haunt his restless ("Trotter") and fugitive spirit. The other extended symbol draws the analogy of a game of checkers to Harry's own life. His obsession to dominate is graphically portrayed:

They played the game steadily until of eight checkers on the black and red squares, six were Harry's. He grinned eagerly, confidently. Gradually he had driven her into a corner. Wherever she moved he had her. His organization had been perfect. Not a single false move and now he had her. Wherever she moved she was bound to lose one checker. She studied the board. He leaned back, grinning, making a swaggering motion with his hand. He had her.

He looked at the six checkers he had manipulated perfectly, each one having a definite part in the trap he had set. . . . Now he had complete control of the game's course. Things going his way. Every move thought out and making absolutely sure he couldn't be beaten. Vera moved reluctantly and he quickly jumped her, removing the checker from the board. She had only one left and the game was practically over. He considered the board and the checkers, ready for the last move, but in reality thinking of the board as his own life and the life around him, his interest reaching a high pitch until it became for him no longer a game of checkers. He had the issue, the opposition, in the hollow of his hand. He felt fine. [12]

Throughout the book there is a gentle play of irony. Harry never understands his own disposition. He does not realize that his love for his wife Vera is really a continuance of his affection for his mother. His story of his drinking grandfather, "the skeleton in the family closet," [13] is an ironical prelude to his own death while dealing in liquor. His recollection of his father's painting, considered by the Art Committee as remarkable for an untutored artist yet unsuitable for showing in the annual exhibition, is an

[26]

ironical prefiguration of Harry's own refusal to conform to rules. The grand party he threw for the "ward heelers, big guys . . . the dukes in politics, women and wine and whiskey and food, slabs of it, gobs of it, truck loads of beer, champagne," [14] in order to prove himself stronger and more influential than the murdered Cosantino, serves only to reveal his inner emptiness to himself and to betray his insecurity to his business enemies. Some of the names of characters, like Anna ("grace") and Eva ("life-giving") convey a subtle, even if unintentional, touch of irony.

Finally, this first published book demonstrates clearly Callaghan's early ideas about style. Years later he described his feelings at that time about writing:

I remember deciding that the root of the trouble with writing was that poets and storywriters used language to evade, to skip away from the object, because they could never bear to face the thing freshly and see it freshly for what it was in itself. A kind of double talk; one thing always seen in terms of another thing. Criticism? A dreary metaphor. The whole academic method! Of course there were lines like *Life's but a walking shadow*. . . . Just the same, I'd be damned if the glory of literature was in the metaphor. Besides, it was not a time for the decorative Renaissance flight into simile. Tell the truth cleanly. Weren't the consequences of fraudulent pretending plain to anyone who would look around? [15]

In spite of himself, however, Callaghan's *Strange Fugitive* reflects the influence of realists who enriched their own narratives with figures of speech. As the very title indicates, the novel is based on a metaphor of flight that is expressed in language reminiscent of Flaubert's *Madame Bovary*:

Always he got back to Vera. He had left her, and was going further and further away so that now he was without passion for her and was anxious for new experiences in strange places. There was a world where he could be alone in his own life, but now she had become a strong thought, a magnet, and all his new thoughts returned finally to her.[16]

Depicted "as a man who in other days on barbaric islands would have been a tribal chief," Harry does in fact flee to the barbaric jungle of gangsterism where he wages tribal war with primitive ruthlessness. Like Emma Bovary, too, he has a romantic ideal— his youthful sweetheart, Grace Leonard: "he imagined, in her, all the sympathetic qualities that might have made him happy. She was part of a background for all his emotional experiences, a memory that assisted him in his love-making with the big woman, Julie Roberts, and in his practical life with Vera." [17] Russian novelists are also echoed in the story. In Harry's delineation the Dostoevskian duality of aggressiveness is combined with the desire for security. Like Tolstoy's Anna Karenina, Harry learns that the wages of sin is death. His wheel of life is stopped in an ironical repetition of the method by which he himself had murdered Cosantino. Just as Anna watched the wheel of the railway carriage under which she threw herself, Harry "saw the wheels of the car going round and round. . . . slowly and he was dead."

Yet if such foreign influences are evident, there is also a distinctively individual style exhibited in *Strange Fugitive*. There are actually relatively few literary ornaments: a rapid, reportorial exposition, short, simple sentences with few adjectives, a colloquial dialogue which is hard and fresh and catches the rhythm of North American speech, and compact descriptive passages which often focus on apparently trivial but really significant details. The effect thus achieved, although occasionally monotonous and flat in its pedestrian quality, is thoroughly appropriate to the theme and point of view of the characters as well as consistent with Callaghan's concept of prose as an instrument of aesthetic purpose.

CHAPTER 2

A Native Argosy

CALLAGHAN'S initial collection of short stories, *A Native Argosy* (1929), is arranged in three sections. The first, entitled "American Made," contains fourteen short stories, many of which had already appeared in magazines. The second, "An Autumn Penitent," and the last, "In His Own Country," are novellas of about a hundred pages each.

I "American Made"

For Callaghan "American" means North American—above the Mason-Dixon Line. Eleven of the tales in "American Made" are set in a city with streets recognizably Torontonian—although the city is not mentioned by name—and the remaining three take place in small Ontario communities: "Ancient Lineage" in Campbellford near Peterborough;[1] "A Country Passion" and "Amuck in the Bush" in the town of Collingwood on Georgian Bay, which is also the setting for "An Autumn Penitent" and "In His Own Country." Despite such "native" locales, however, these stories are not parochially Canadian; many of the urban ones were actually inspired by New York. They all represent aspects of humanity which are universal.

In themes, too, *A Native Argosy* carries a cargo that is representative of the aspirations and frustrations of ordinary North Americans during the twenties. Callaghan once remarked, "I have never sat down to write a book to carry out a theme."[2] Yet there are certain perceptions about human life that keep recurring, not only in this volume, but in his later work. Central to these is the view that "man has possibilities to realize himself on a much fuller scale than he does. But the world seems to be full of frustrated people —people who in some mean or desperate way get blocked off from being what they should be."[3]

Many of the stories in *A Native Argosy* are concerned with family relationships and love. Like Tolstoy, whose works he had read thoroughly as a young man, Callaghan has an image of humanity which considers love, the need to love and be loved, a fundamental trait in human nature, and the Sermon on the Mount as a desirable guide to life. It is perhaps not accidental that virtually the only literary allusion in the book is to *Anna Karenina*.[4] For the opening line of that novel, "Happy families are all alike; every unhappy family is unhappy in its own way," has relevance to many of Callaghan's short stories. Also inherent in many of these tales is the concept of life expressed by Tolstoy in *My Confession:* "It is possible to live only as long as life intoxicates us; a soon as we are sober again we see that it is all a delusion, a stupid delusion." Reminiscent of Swift's "sublime and refined point of felicity, called, the possession of being well deceived," this intoxication with life may come in *A Native Argosy* from pride of family, as in "Ancient Lineage," or from a romantic dream, as in "A Regret for Youth," "A Girl With Ambition," "A Cocky Young Man," "A Wedding Dress," "Settling Down," and "In His Own Country." Yet in the inevitable clash between such dreams and reality, unless the individual involved can preserve a sense of dignity, his end is pathetic, if not tragic.

The characters who illustrate these themes in "American Made" frequently belong to what has been called the world "of Moronia." [5] Two of the pieces dealing with life in country towns illustrate particularly this description. The central figures in "A Country Passion"—forty-five year old Jim Cline, with a multiple jail record, and his mentally retarded sweetheart, sixteen year old Ettie Corley—reveal the frustration of subnormal intelligences, yearning for love and companionship but thwarted by society. In "Amuck in the Bush" a "hunkie" lumberyard worker, Gus Rapp, fired for trying to hit his boss, Sid Walton, with a plank (an incident repeated in *Strange Fugitive*) broods over a scheme for revenge. Following Mrs. Walton and her daughter into the bush, he attacks them in a fury of rage, alcohol and frustration. Confused about his own motivation, he is intellectually incapable of coping with this emotional crisis in his life.

Nor are some of the city folk, although more sophisticated than their rural counterparts, able to cope any more effectively with their problems. Workers, and even managers, in shops and department stores, married couples trying to adjust, deserted wives and husbands, jobless misfortunates, reporters and priests are all united, together with their rustic brethren, by a common humanity. As an erstwhile reporter Callaghan is keenly aware that there is often little difference beween the educated and the illiterate, the wealthy and the poor, in their ability to face and solve these routine problems of life—misunderstandings and quarrels, disillusionments and frustrating maladjustments.

The fact that many of the broad themes are repeated and that many of the characters are alike in their semi-articulateness gives a kind of unity to *A Native Argosy*. But any attempt to classify its tales as stories of action, or character, or setting, or idea or emotional effect is unlikely to be rewarding. For their qualities are not definable in this stereotyped way. As Sean O'Faolain notes, "What one enjoys in a short story is a special distillation of personality, a unique sensibility which has recognized and selected at once a subject that, above all other subjects, is of value to the writer's temperament." [6]

This kind of selection is, in fact, typical of Callaghan's own method. Choosing from his mental album of characters one of particular interest, he ponders this person until he is satisfied that his conclusions about the imagined figure are right. He then devises the proper pattern to express this character, and designs a situation in which the way the character acts and thinks will reveal everything about him to the reader. There is no set formula for such tales. "You don't write stories like those deliberately. You write those stories out of a kind of feeling for life and people drained through whatever peculiar intellectual system you have, or whatever kind of a heart you have." [7]

Callaghan's "intellectual system" during the period in which he was writing the pieces in *A Native Argosy* was influenced largely by American writers. At times his stories are superficially reminiscent of Stephen Crane's *Whilomville Stories* (1900)—in their intense perceptions of actual town happenings—as well as of the tales of Sherwood Anderson and Hemingway. Like them, Callaghan in his early tales implicitly rejects the great illusions of North American civilization, its puerile optimism and evasion of hard facts. He gives a faithful, detailed depiction of the everyday world in language that is spare and simple. His characters are common-place and talk in bare, clipped, colloquial speech. His material, like that of Hemingway, is often drawn from a reporter's world. Like Hemingway, he portrays a mood or situation by a series of apparently trivial details which are synthesized in a significant yet unobtrusive symbol.

The grotesques of *Winesburg, Ohio* have their counterparts in Callaghan's stories. His characters reflect a kind of expressionism, a certain looseness of form that represents "lives flowing past each other" yet implies an underlying pattern of rhythm. They also act in ways that may seem perverse and childish to the reader, but paradoxically enough they often do so for moral reasons. Despite such similarities, however, Callaghan's style—contrary to popular misconception—is different from that of either of his older con-temporaries with whose writings his early work has so often been linked. Anderson, preoccupied with the increasing mechanization and standardization of the modern world, frequently generalizes without concrete illustration, and sometimes even resorts to cari-catures in order to point his thesis. Although he shows the same sympathy with the problems of people, Callaghan is usually more objective than Anderson and his most explicit comments on his themes are contained in his titles.

Five years junior to Hemingway, Callaghan was too young to have experience in the First World War. Nor had he travelled when he published *A Native Argosy.* He has no tales of wounded and bitter veterans, disillusioned expatriates in Europe, bull fight-ers or big game hunters. Although proficient in sports, he is not absorbed by the youthful values implied in such participation. His characters are not obsessed with the cult of the athletic and the outdoors, nor is their physical courage constantly being put to the proof. Unlike Hemingway, Callaghan has no devil-may-care, ruth-less, hard-drinking stoic heroes, living by a code and portrayed against exotic backgrounds, to fire the imagination. Nor has he an intermediary narrator like Nick Adams with whom the reader can sympathetically identify himself. The dramatic rigor, the violence and the frequently harsh emotional tone of Hemingway's nerv-ously electric portrayal are absent. In marked contrast are the wistful lyric quality, the Celtic fancy, the supremely ironic point of view—which can be compassionate or detached—and the intuitive insight into the significance of the minutiae of ordinary life which characterize Callaghan's presentation. Moral rather than physical courage is his concern. His tales have a subtle, underlying psychological tension which draws the reader forward. Their individual flavor may be recognized by an examination of various stories in *A Native Argosy*.

The theme of "A Country Passion," the initial story in "American Made" has already been noted. Originally printed in the March, 1928 issue of *transition,* this story was the first of fourteen to appear in successive years in J. Edward O'Brien's annual *The Best Short Stories,* which ceased publication in 1941, the year after O'Brien's death. The brief ironic action of "A Country Passion" is imaginatively and compellingly rendered through the senses and slow-witted consciousness of Jim Cline. His genuine love for the backward Ettie Corley is evidenced in his desire to marry her, his provision of food and coal for her family, and his purchase of proper clothes for her to wear. This honest charity is incongruously rewarded by the minister's refusal to marry the couple, and then later by his irritable admission of his ineffectuality to aid Jim in the face of the charge of seduction and abduction laid against him. The latter's puzzlement in his cell over this dilemma is conveyed in language which illustrates Callaghan's mastery of "flat" characterization and the rhetoric that goes with it:

He had almost hit upon an idea that would be a solution for everything. Everybody knew it would be best for Ettie to marry him, and Ettie wanted to, and he could go to work, but the people who had arrested him couldn't understand it. Fiercely indignant, he felt himself getting excited. If he could get out he could explain his idea to everybody and get people behind him.

But his escape brings only recapture for himself and makes inevitable Ettie's confinement in an institution. Just as Jim had pulled "a broken picket from the scantling and tossed it out on the road" without any attempt at repair, likewise society rejects rather than reclaims its defectives. His bewilderment when his moral decision leads to frustration and suffering enlists the sympathy of the reader.

In "Last Spring They Came Over," two "English-made" brothers, Alfred and Harry Bowles, sons "of a Baptist minister whose family was too large for his salary," are described. Alfred, the first to arrive in Canada, becomes a reporter with a Toronto newspaper:

The night editor took a fancy to him because of the astounding puerility of his political opinions. Alfred was always willing to talk pompously of the British Empire policing the world and about all Catholics being aliens, and the future of Ireland and Canada resting with the Orangemen.

Then Harry joins Alfred and secures a position on the same paper. Although different in temperament, they live together blissfully in their own ingenuous male world of derbies and canes, of ritualistic beer toasts, of conversational clichés and of dreams of travel to other "colonies" of the Empire. Within the year both are fired, Harry dies of pneumonia and Alfred drifts away from the city.

Inspired by Callaghan's actual acquaintance with two such types,[8] the fictional delineation of these whimsical characters is appropriately journalistic, since it is presented from the point of view of a fellow reporter. The child-like naïveté of the brothers is contrasted with the hard-boiled practical joking of the newspapermen, whom Callaghan somewhat sentimentally stereotypes as sympathetic and generous beneath their cynical shell. The Englishmen's fanciful world of dreams, as symbolized by the great golden temple of the Sikhs at Amritsar, is ironically juxtaposed with the everyday world of newspaper headlines—fires, accidents and police court cases.

"A Predicament" and "A Regret for Youth" are the two pieces included in that issue of *Scribner's Magazine* of July, 1928, which by a special green band across its orange-yellow cover heralded a "New Fiction Star—Morley Callaghan, with two unusual stories." Inside the magazine this young Canadian was enthusiastically introduced to the public by the editors:

His strength, individuality, and versatility will, we believe, place him in the front rank of the younger writers. It will be remembered that on the other occasion when we presented two stories in the same number the writer was Ernest Hemingway. Mr. Callaghan has contributed to the little magazines, but he has never before appeared in a periodical of general circulation.[9]

"A Predicament" is an intensely perceptive and human story of the dilemma of "the youngest priest at the Cathedral." Such a character has always had a special appeal for Callaghan: "there have been young priests in the world for 4000 years. They stand on the threshold of a spiritual voyage, and I guess I feel touched, wondering if they're going to make it." [10] Hearing confessions on a Saturday afternoon, Father Francis is confronted on the other side of the confessional panel by a drunken man who thinks him a conductor on a streetcar. Undecided as to whether to report the incident to his superior or have the man thrown out and thus risk unfavorable publicity, the conscientious young priest reluctantly determines to handle the situation himself. But he evades the issue temporarily and compromises by hearing a woman's confession first. Ironically her sin is deception—mostly in the form of white lies, which, as he comments, "may not endanger your soul, but they lead to something worse."

Father Francis' predicament is vividly portrayed by a series of concrete details: his nervous gestures of rubbing "his smooth cheek with his hand" and "his shoulder blades uneasily against the back of the confessional," of wiping his lips, clearing his throat and feeling his heart beat unevenly as he breaks into a sweat; his recollections of "drunkenness, the overindulgence of an appetite, the drunken state. Scholastic psychology"; his inability to concentrate and his attempt to calm himself by saying three "Our Fathers" and "Hail Marys"; and his vain hope, as he tries to push back the panel without making a grating noise, that the man may have gone. The situation is developed suspensefully and sympathetically. The reader shares with the youthful priest his consternation and then his initial happiness at having disposed of the drunk by speaking to him like a conductor: "Step lively there; this is King and Yonge. Do you want to go past your stop?" Equally understandable are Father Francis' subsequent remorse that he "had descended to artifice in the confessional to save himself from embarrassment" and his desire to settle his own conscience before he decides whether he will "tell the bishop." This ending is ironical in its subtle repetition of the young priest's attempt to solve problems himself without seeking help from experienced superiors, as well as in his continuing self-evasion.

In "A Regret for Youth" very different emotions are represented. Mrs. Jerry Austin, a plump deserted wife of thirty, dreams romantically of winning the love of Mr. Jarvis, a jaunty youth eight years her junior. Their only common bond, however, is their mutual antipathy to their landlady, Mrs. Oddy, and her husband. The anodyne for Mrs. Austin's loneliness and frustration, for her desperate yearning to appear youthful and feel desired, is the delusion that Jarvis may come to love her. Her hours before the mirror fixing her hair, adjusting her corset and carrying on imaginary conversations convey the poignancy of her position. Ironically and realistically Jarvis' farewell reveals his genuine regard for her, but not in the amorous role which she has envisioned in her fairy mirror: "You're a good sport . . . I've got an aunt just like you."

In the August, 1928, number of *Scribner's Magazine* appeared "Soldier Harmon," the story of a big, slow-witted prizefighter. Although Joe Harmon enjoys the inner excitement and emotional release of the knockout blow, and likes dressing "smartly in form-fitting clothes, a purple handkerchief tucked carelessly in his breast-pocket," he has grown "tired of sparring and road-work and even watching bouts, because he was interested only in the big moment in a fight and everything led up to it." He would rather have an ordinary job, but his sweetheart Molly, his trainer Doc Barnes, and his parents selfishly push him to advance his professional career. Nor can he communicate with them his real feelings except in his imaginary conversations. Matched with the heavyweight champion, he knocks out Harry Greb "in the third round but the bell saved him." Although Joe is beaten, he remembers the fight with pleasure for this one moment of triumph. In his next bout he topples his opponent, Tommy Goldie:

The referee had counted six when Goldie rolled over and got up on one knee. Slightly bewildered he watched him, then rushed across the ring and pushed aside the referee, eager to hit Goldie. The time-keeper stopped counting. The referee held on to Joe, trying to push him away. Joe could think only of Goldie attempting to get up after he had landed satisfactorily and knocked him down.

Saved by this technicality, Goldie comes back to win the fight by knocking Joe through the ropes.

The reader is left to decide whether Joe deliberately allows himself to be beaten. His defeat, however, does free Joe from the ambitions of his friends. Ironically, his predicament is paralleled by his relationship with his little bull pup. He wants it to play at his whim and develop the appearance of a real fighter:

> . . . he was worried because it looked as if the pup's legs weren't going to bow sufficiently to give him a really ferocious appearance. He grabbed the legs at the joints, hunching up the shoulders. He pulled down the lower lip, showing strong teeth. The dog liked it and looked splendid as long as he could hold the position.

The ambivalence of the conclusion and its suggestive final image aptly illustrate the complex and contradictory aspects of human personality.

The central figure of "A Princely Affair" is a former army captain who has become manager of haberdashery in a large department store. Married to an English wife with a "fondness for theatricals, and social connections," Bill Oakley is himself a romantic dreamer. His temperament is swiftly presented in the opening situation as he studies through half-closed eyes a hunting picture on a calendar in a barber shop:

> The huntsmen made him think of his wife Nora. The statesman, with the bulging forehead and long formidable nose, belonged to the same tradition. The huntsman, his wife, and the statesman; or his wife, the huntsman, and the statesman; or his wife, the statesman, and the huntsman, different combinations, all very good, all part of a fine tradition.

In this paragraph the deteriorating triangular relationship of himself, his wife, and her socially prominent escorts is suggested. For Bill "had often talked of taking up fox-hunting," and as the narrative opens his wife Nora has just made newspaper headlines by dancing three times with His Highness, Captain Albert, at a ball. As Nora follows the royal entourage to Montreal, pauses in New York, allegedly to play "a small part in a big company," and finally sends a letter from Spain, Bill's changing attitude toward her and this "fine tradition" is subtly and ironically unfolded. His increasing disillusionment is paralleled by the progressive decline in his personal tidiness and material prosperity. From the *double entente* of the title to the very end there is a constant play of irony. Bill's initial excitement and pride in his wife's popularity is soon succeeded by irritability at her neglect of household duties. His uneasiness at her leaving home and his lonely and half-hearted approbation of her social success are evident as he reads her "note in the kitchen, the envelope resting on a tin of canned food on the table, and tried to feel enthusiastic but his heart was beating too loudly." His growing surliness at Nora's failure to write regularly reveals his repressed awareness of her actual status and of the fact that he is being cuckolded:

He expected her to write and ask for money, but days passed, and he avoided thinking about it. The last time he went over to the jewelry department to see Steiner he began by explaining pompously that his wife was having an extraordinary success and an account of it should be in the local papers. Then he talked suddenly about women who managed to live on easy street for next to nothing, arguing excitedly with Steiner about such women.

In a reckless, romantic gesture to reassure himself by buying Nora an expensive ermine wrap matching one in a picture she had sent, Bill, who is somehow reminiscent of dull Charles Bovary in Flaubert's *Madame Bovary*, mortgages his home and moves to a cheap apartment. His wife's effusive yet evasive reply to this generous impulse is the cause of his final disillusionment. The department store is opening a new branch in the West and his request to move there is granted by his manager J. C. Carlton. Bill's final words, "The wife is in Spain. His Highness and his party are there," and his reflection on them in the concluding flat but expressive sentence bring the story full cycle back to its opening:

He spoke deliberately, and didn't intend Carlton to answer him. He walked away quickly, glad that he had said it, fiercely insistent that no one should say anything to him. The department was gone. What he told Carlton belonged to a tradition. It should all go together.

In "Ancient Lineage," a sensitive portrayal of *déclassé* descendants of a famous pioneer family, Callaghan's descriptive passages are subtly evocative. Young Mr. Flaherty from the University Historical Club visits the village home, heavy with decayed grandeur, of old Mrs. Rower and her unmarried daughter: "framed photographs of dead conservative politicians, the group of military men hanging over the old-fashioned piano, the faded greenish wall paper and the settee in the corner." Against this pathetically shabby setting the family's illustrious past is ironically juxtaposed. The daughter, Hilda, "a large woman of about forty" and "primly conscious of lineal superiority," must charge twenty-five cents for a copy of her brief account of the family's part in the early military settlement.

Yet as the fat and unattractive Hilda warms to the recollections of her ancestors a "soft light came into her eyes and her lips were moist. . . . she was talking slowly, lazily, relaxing in her chair, a warm fluid oozing through her veins, exhausting but satisfying her." Watching this transformation with embarrassment Flaherty withdraws to his hotel:

Half-way down the path Mr. Flaherty turned. She was standing in the doorway, partly shadowed by the tall trees, bright moonlight filtering through leaves touching soft lines on her face and dark hair. . . . For a long time he lay awake in the fresh, cool bed, the figure of the woman whose ancient lineage had taken the place of a lover in her life, drifting into his thoughts and becoming important while he watched on the wall the pale moonlight that had softened the lines of her face, and wondered if it was still shining on her bed, and on her throat, and on her contented, lazily relaxed body.

The contrast between the virile past and the sterile present is dramatized and humanized by Callaghan's adroit employment of the imagery of love and moonlight, and the reader's imagination responds sympathetically to this final image of faded splendor.

A dream ironically realized is the theme of "A Girl With Ambition," which, as Callaghan's first published story, appeared in *This Quarter* in 1926. Mary Ross, young attractive blonde, is ambitious for a stage career. Leaving public school at sixteen, she "worked for two weeks with a cheap chorus at La Plaza, quitting when her stepmother heard the girls were a lot of toughs." As cashier in a department store Mary meets a summer employee, Harry Brown, who responds sympathetically to her aspirations: "she looked up to him because he was going to be a lawyer. Harry admired her ambition but was a little shy. He thought she knew too much for him." The friendship of these two teenagers of different temperaments, backgrounds, and vocabularies, is presented with insight and understanding. For although they see each other only infrequently after Harry returns to school, he continues to symbolize for Mary what is respectable in life: "Thinking of how he liked her made her feel a little better than the girls she knew." And though Mary is obviously becoming increasingly dissolute, Harry, too, is drawn toward her and enthusiastically impressed when she gets a position as a dancer in a musical comedy.

This job, which only lasts two weeks, is actually the peak of Mary's frustrated career. "Even her stepmother was pleased because it was a respectable company that a girl didn't need to be ashamed of." Callaghan's use of the word "respectable," constantly repeated throughout the story to point up the contrast between Mary's world and that of Harry, is here deliberate and ironical. For to celebrate this occasion Mary goes to a party with Wilfred Barnes, the grocer's son, "playing strip poker until four a.m." The inevitable reversal of this apparent triumph and the disparity between her shoddy world of easy living and the stodgier but more stable one of respectability are symbolized in her meeting with Harry and a friend of his at a roller rink:

She was late. Harry was trying to roller skate with another fellow, fair haired, long legged, wearing large glasses. They had never roller skated before but were trying to appear unconcerned and dignified. They looked very funny because every one else on the floor was free and easy, willing to start a fight. Mary got her skates on but the old music box stopped and the electric sign under it flashed, reverse. The music started again. The skaters turned and went the opposite way. Harry and his friend skated off the floor because they couldn't cut corners with the left foot.

Even her marriage to Wilfred Barnes, following his jail sentence for stealing, which was "only two months because his parents were very respectable people," does not dim Mary's hopes to be successful on the stage. But a brief engagement with a circus and later a small part (at the very La Plaza where she had begun her stage career) which she is forced to give up because of pregnancy, ironically bring her ambition full cycle.

The final scene is a paradoxical realization of her aspirations. Riding one day with her husband delivering groceries, she suddenly recognizes Harry:

Mary sat on the wagon seat. Three young fellows and a woman were sitting up on a veranda opposite the wagon. She saw Harry looking at her and vaguely wondered how he got there. She didn't want him to see that she was going to have a baby. Leaning on the veranda rail, he saw that her slimness had passed into the shapelessness of her pregnancy and he knew why she had been kept off the stage that night at the La Plaza. She sat erect and strangely dignified on the seat of the grocery wagon, uncomfortable when he turned away.

In this domestic drama the girl with ambition finally holds the center of the stage which she had so eagerly sought and has for an audience the one man whose attention signifies respect for her. Unconsciously she achieves in her conventional role of expectant mother the respectability, distinction and dignity which so long have eluded her as a juvenile delinquent.

"A Cocky Young Man" introduces the reader to a delightfully whimsical poseur as seen through the eyes of a fellow reporter, Patterson. Reminiscent in some ways of the brothers in "Last Spring They Came Over," Hendricks takes a job with the *Morning Empire*. With his large black fedora, knobby cane and little moustache he radiates an air of easy assurance and importance which brings him the nickname of "The Duke" and perplexes his superiors. After an interview with Bassler, the editor, Hendricks gets a special assignment to investigate various aspects of bootlegging in the city. As he later admits to Patterson, the sensational articles were all faked: "When I first suggested it to Bassler he told me what he had been trying to get for years. . . . so I simply confirmed his opinion."

Hendricks' intuitive understanding of human nature (from editors to elevator operators), his vast range of knowledge of mundane matters (from salads to Indian paintings), and his urge for constantly changing horizons make plausible his absurd desire to document human experience: "He didn't want to be an author, just write one book something like Anna Karenina."

Callaghan's narrative technique skilfully underlines the central character's restless spirit as well as his natural charm. The story begins on a lakeboat coming back from Niagara at sunset. From the vistas of grapevines and orchards the reader moves easily—in Hardy fashion—along with Hendricks, Patterson and his girl into the activity of the city newspaper. The story concludes one evening three months later with the same three figures at the railway station as Hendricks departs to try harvesting out west. In the opening he sought the company of Patterson and his girl and at the end he is sought by them. As he was "leaning over the rail enjoying the sunset" then, so now he is "leaning out the window." Even the subject of salad comes up again. This device of repetition with variation, as well as the images of transportation, appropriately suggests the eager, searching and winsome temperament of the cocky young man.

"Amuck in the Bush," which appeared in *The American Caravan* of 1927, explores the perceptions of Gus Rapp, a lumberyard laborer. Presented in the language of this "hunkie," his laziness in the drowsy heat of the sun, his sullen and vindictive response to his boss's urging, his resentment at being fired and his attempt to palliate his wounded dignity by drinking squirrel whiskey evoke an image of a mindless and passionate animal. Watching his boss's wife set off with her daughter Anna to go berry picking, Gus is filled with confused emotions, with hate for Sid Walton and lust for Walton's wife:

He sat on the front steps for twenty minutes, his head in his hands, spitting at a bug crawling on the picket walk and thinking about grabbing and hiding the kid that always became Mrs. Walton when he thought about it very much. "That'll make Walton sweat all right," he thought, and got up quickly, happy to go swinging along the road beyond the town to the berry-patch in the bush. He thought about stealing the kid but liked following Mrs. Walton. She had full red lips and a lot of black hair bunched over her ears.

As he follows them to the fringe of the woods Gus's excitement rises, his primitive instincts responding appropriately to the uncivilized setting. In order to bring out Gus's earthy quality, Callaghan uses imagery that is strong and sensuous. In the warm afternoon sun, the brownish green leaves falling in the path, Mrs. Walton moving "slowly with strong stride, her wide-brimmed hat flapping regularly," Anna playfully hiding behind the huge rounded rocks, the berries "black and heavy . . . fell with a soft thud in the bottom of the pail." Gus's surprise assault on Mrs. Walton is ironically as abortive as was his underhand attack on her husband. In the scuffle, goaded by the little girl's screams and a painful bite from her mother, he fires his gun, "grazing her forehead" and "gashing her cheek." Frustrated in his revenge, Gus flies in panic through the bush.

The reader's antipathy now changes to pity for, and even sympathy with, this befuddled man. The primitive Gus is as ineffectual in the habitat of animals as he was in a social milieu. Banging into trees, clumsily climbing vines, terrified at the lapping of lake water in the darkness and eventually weary, hungry and baffled by his predicament he is inextricably drawn back to civilization to be captured and roped to a lamppost like a savage beast by hostile fellow humans:

He leaned his weight forward on the ropes, staring hard at the bat that swooped and darted around the light overhead. The police car came along deliberately and they had no trouble with Gus. The car turned around and as Gus got in, the kids yelled and threw pebbles and sticks at him.

The bat exemplifies Callaghan's subtle yet complex use of symbol. Prehistoric creature of darkness, perplexed by light and associated in literature with the devil himself, this rodent is mammalian but able to fly. It thus suggests man's duality—his predominantly animal nature combined with the inherent capability for soaring aspiration. The bat's apparently purposeless darting around the light parallels the aimlessness of Gus's thoughts contrasted with the potential of illuminating intelligence.

In "A Wedding Dress" the yearning of a respectable spinster to look attractive on her wedding day leads her to steal an expensive dress. Disappointed in the plainness of cheaper materials and prompted by the sneering sarcasm of a salesgirl, Lena Schwartz examines an expensive gown:

She liked the feeling it left in the tips of her fingers. She stood alone at the rack, toying with the material, her mind playing with thoughts she guiltily enjoyed. She imagined herself wantonly attractive in the dress, slyly watched by men with bold thoughts as she walked down the street with Sam, who would be nervously excited when he drew her into some corner and put his hands on her shoulders. Her heart began to beat heavily. She wanted to walk out of the room and over to the escalator but could not think clearly. Her fingers were carelessly drawing the dress into her wide coat sleeve, the dress disappearing steadily and finally slipping easily from the hanger, drawn into her wide sleeve.

Lena immediately regrets her dishonest impulse. In her disturbed imagination her fiancé, Sam Hilton, seems to be "drifting away from her. She would have gone back with the dress but did not know how to go about it." She is arrested and spends the night in jail like a common criminal. Turned over to the custody of Sam, who has agreed to pay for the dress, she is given a suspended sentence.

Callaghan's treatment, with its particularity of descriptive detail and suggestive dialogue, is sensitive and compassionate. Lena's glamorous dreams of seductiveness contrast ironically with her actual appearance in the stolen garment during the court scene: "the dress too short and hanging loosely on her thin body." The author compels in the reader a sympathetic understanding of the romantic yearning which prompts her temporary kleptomania, of the humiliation attending arrest and trial, and finally of the subdued sense of shame which this circumspect spinster feels as "Sam gravely took her arm and they went out to be quietly married."

"An Escapade" conveys the complex feelings of a Roman Catholic who surreptitiously attends a Protestant service. Mrs. Rose Carey, "good-looking for forty-two," is "bothered by her own shyness" about going to hear a popular preacher of whom "all her bridge friends were talking." Callaghan rapidly develops this vague uneasiness of conscience into an intense inner conflict in which not only religious orthodoxy but even moral issues are involved. For as though to remind her of the pitfalls in the path of those who stray from the fold, a series of disturbing incidents befalls Mrs. Carey. At the entrance of the theater, where the Reverend John Simpson is holding Sunday evening service, she is accosted by an odd fellow:

She stopped abruptly, nervously watching the little man with the long nose and green sweater, pacing up and down in front of the entrance, waving his hands. He saw her hesitating and came close to her. He had on a funny flat black hat, and walked with his toes turned way out. "Step lively, lady," he muttered, wagging his head at her.

Frightened by this Crazy Dick (who by the similarity of his performance to that of a circus barker reduces the religious service to the status of a side-show), Mrs. Carey is reassured by a distinguished-looking gentleman. To her annoyance this new companion sits down beside her in the theater. Unable to concentrate on the minister's sermon concerning an after-life, her mind wanders to a recollection of a trivial argument with her husband. In the unfamiliar religious setting she feels "slightly ashamed, and out of place." When her companion is moved to tears by the clergyman's words, she feels a surge of compassion, and oblivious to other listeners speaks comfortingly to him until those in front turn angrily around:

She became embarrassed, and leaned back in her seat, very dignified, and looked directly ahead till aware that the man was holding her hand. Startled, she twitched it nervously, but he didn't notice. His eyes were still moist. His thoughts seemed so far away. She reflected it could do no harm to let him hold her hand a moment, if it helped him.

This apparently innocent gesture of sympathy, which symbolically parallels her self-indulgent desire to attend the Protestant service, has multiple ramifications as she

. . . glanced curiously at the gray-haired man, who didn't look at her but still held her hand. He was good-looking and a feeling she had not had for years was inside her, her hand had suddenly become so sensitive. She closed her eyes. She looked directly at him. He had put away the handkerchief and now was smiling sadly. Uneasily, she avoided his eyes, firmly removing her hand, as she stood up to sing the last hymn.

Her cheeks were warm. She tried to stop thinking altogether. It was necessary to leave at once only she had to squeeze his knees to reach the aisle.

Outside the theater the snow, which earlier was falling lazily "giving her, in her thick warm coat, a fine feeling of self-indulgence," is now "driving along on a wind." Turning her back on her still lingering companion, she heads for the cathedral. "One light was over the church door. The congregation had come out half an hour ago, and she felt lonely walking in the dark toward the single light." Inside the cathedral she prays hard in an attempt to dismiss the thoughts of what has happened in the theater.

This psychological rendering of the inner life of Mrs. Rose Carey (whose very name suggests both passionate love and sympathetic concern) is sensitive and intuitive. Her original curiosity, her guilty misgivings and restlessness, her warm compassion for her sorrowful companion and later her spontaneous, sensuous response toward him, her honest respectability, her guilty feeling that she has somehow betrayed both her Church and her impotent husband, and her longing for peace of mind, are all delicately portrayed.

The remaining two stories of "American Made" yet to be discussed—since they are not included in *Morley Callaghan's Stories* (1959)—will be briefly treated. The first of these is a dramatic record of "The Life of Sadie Hall." With remarkable economy and psychological insight Callaghan gives the background of this juvenile delinquent. His two opening sentences encompass her girlhood past: "Sadie Hall was ten years old when her father went away, leaving her and her brother Shelley with an Aunt Hilda Martin. Sadie could not remember her mother." The next two sentences indicate Aunt Hilda's mercenary and uncharitable nature. Swiftly Sadie's adolescence is depicted: her "careless laugh," increasing "impudence" in school, "wild reckless ways" and popularity with the boys. At sixteen she has a job and takes a room of her own "where she could entertain her friends." The remarks about her by Uncle Pete ("she's a vixen") and by a former school friend ("She sure makes a guy feel free and easy") are revealing.

Callaghan's careful presentation of Sadie, as though from the viewpoint of a social worker trying to piece together *ex post facto* the events leading up to an inevitable tragedy, is suddenly focused on her final twenty-four hour period. The reader, already filled with foreboding, follows with horrified anticipation Sadie's hilarious return from a wild week-end party. Aunt Hilda's concluding sentiments, moreover, form an ironic comment on Sadie's sad case: "She would not talk about it, having known from the first that Sadie would come to a bad end. She told the reporters not to dare mention her own name in the papers."

The final and longest story in this section of *A Native Argosy,* "Settling Down," is basically a combination of two themes already developed in previous stories of this volume. Full of echoes of incidents from Callaghan's own youth, the story has as its hero Burgess (Burg) Morgan, a male counterpart of Mary Ross in "A Girl With Ambition." Burg also resembles Hendricks in "A Cocky Young Man." Burlesque shows, mining in a Northern Ontario town, prairie harvesting and journalism are all experience for this aspiring young writer. Like Hendricks, he writes a sensational story on bootlegging. This article may have originally been suggested to Callaghan by Hemingway's "full-column survey of the role which Canadians and Canadian liquor were playing in the violation of American prohibition, in the *Star Weekly* of June 5, 1920." [11] After being fired from virtually all of his jobs, Burg achieves a rather comically incongruous success as a magazine salesman: "Sometimes Burg read specimens of his own prose to the women and they liked the specimens so much they asked him to have a cup of tea. These were good moments for Burg. After the tea they patriotically bought the magazine, if they had the money." Still dreaming of becoming a famous writer, he reflects with ironical self-delusion that this "shack-tapping" is "like building your own public."

II *"An Autumn Penitent"*

The second part of *A Native Argosy* is a novella of ninety-six pages entitled "An Autumn Penitent." Published in *The American Caravan* for 1928, this little epic of unheroic small-town life is divided into twelve sections without subtitles. Set near Toronto in Eastmount, a village bypassed by a new highway and high-level bridge that spanned the entire valley, the story begins in summer and ends some six weeks later in mid-September. Its suspenseful action, which starts *in medias res* and moves with imperceptible speed, is dominated by two main occurrences. Although the first of these, a sexual act involving generation, takes place before the present action of the story begins, the reader feels its powerful and ineluctable force long before he learns what it actually is. The second event, a baptism involving regeneration, builds up in anticipation a highly charged atmosphere in which the discovery of the seduction explodes with tremendous impact. Even after the dramatic suicide which follows this *anagnorisis*, interest is sustained through the public gesture of atonement made by the violator to the final subdued movement in which the action returns full cycle to his own hearth.

The central figure, Joe Harding, "plump, soft and a little bald" at forty-seven, is a carpenter who lives with his wife Lottie and sixteen-year-old niece Ellen. The details of Joe's character are drawn with subtle strokes. His physical interest in Ellen and overly protective attitude toward her, his preoccupation with newspaper accounts of police court events and his vicarious emotional involvement in them, and his personal tension as the preacher at the revival meeting thunders the vengeance of God against wilful sinners, all make plausible the eventual discovery that he is responsible for Ellen's pregnancy. Yet he has good qualities which make that discovery a painful shock for Lottie: although not religious himself, he gives freely of his evenings to fix up the barn for the revival meetings, is "sympathetic and good-natured" with his wife and so "willing to humor her whims" that he even agrees to kneel down and pray with her; moreover, "everybody in Eastmount spoke of him as a generous-hearted man." This self-indulgent sinner, responsible by his seduction of his niece for her death and the suicide of his wife, not only conceals his guilt from his fellow villagers but even wins public approval and peace of conscience by reversing an earlier decision and submitting to the ceremony of baptism.

Lottie and Ellen are realistically presented also with a mixture of virtues and foibles. Despite her religious zeal, like Chaucer's Wyf of Bath, Lottie is "out of alle charitee," angry and jealous when she is preceded to the platform by a neighbour who is first to be saved. Her fervent enthusiasm for baptism is supplanted for a few days by the excitement of an altercation with a door-to-door magazine salesman. Her response to Ellen's confession and to the knowledge of Joe's guilt, although human enough, is scarcely indicative of a genuine religious faith: "What will people say?" Her desperate resolution of this crisis illustrates both her strength and weakness of character. Nor is the injured Ellen presented as entirely free of all blame for her condition, although the reader is given only a subtle hint of her own responsibility for the seduction in her changed attitude toward Joe: "she no longer encouraged attention but tried to be friendly, reserved, and obedient."

Apart from the student preacher Hodgins, the other characters are typically rural in their earthy outlook, sense of humor and interests. Resembling the people in *Tobacco Road* (1932) and yet less caricatured than Caldwell's yokels, they are forcefully and sympathetically presented here against a background that is charged with religious overtones, and particularly with the ecstatic mood evoked by the evangelical revivalist. Callaghan's ability to participate in the imaginative life of his characters is clearly demonstrated. Although he is set off from them by his articulateness, by his power to describe their trivial concerns and emotional experiences, he conceals this distinction by a deliberate assumption of thought processes and language which are appropriately simple and rustic. By thus reducing the distance between himself and his material he cultivates sympathy with it and brings it to the reader with a directness possible only for an artist willing to efface himself as completely as Callaghan does in this story.

Symbol and irony heighten the drama of "An Autumn Penitent." The theme of generation and regeneration runs throughout. Joe's seduction of Ellen begins a new life in her. The loss of her life is partially atoned for by his own regenerative experience of baptism. In this ceremony, in which he offers himself as a substitute for his wife and niece, he may also be viewed symbolically as the sinner saved by their sacrificial death. The suicide of the two women by drowning is an ironical form of private "total immersion" in which Lottie's arm hooked around Ellen's neck foreshadows the same gesture used by the minister in the public ceremony. Water lapping in the lake, swishing in Lottie's shoe, or "running smoothly and quietly till it seemed a black liquid running through

her mind" is a disturbing background sound. The season of autumn, too, is rich in symbolic suggestion. A time of ripening both
physically and spiritually, it is also a lonely and desolate period.

Joe is the prodigal, the lost sheep for whom those attending the
revival meeting sing the old hymn:

> There were ninety and nine that safely lay
> In the shelter of the fold.
> But one was out on the hill far away . . .

Joe's eventual desire to rejoin the flock brings more joy to the
preacher than "the baptism of the twenty-four good souls whose
faith has made possible the evangelical work in the village." At
the announcement of Joe's decision one star breaks through an
overcast sky. His acceptance of baptism has already been ironically forecast in the preacher's remark to Lottie that "her example
would be a strong influence likely to affect him at the last moment." The gospel songs play an appropriate part in the drama.
"Bringing in the Sheaves" (with its imagery of "sowing in the
shadows" and "waiting for the harvest,/ . . . Tho the loss sustained our spirit often grieves;/ When our weeping's over, He will
bid us welcome,") and the hymn "Shall We Gather at the River?"
(where the saints "shall meet and sorrow never," and at the end of
their pilgrimage "quiver with the melody of peace,") are particularly effective for the reader familiar with the verses of the songs.
These popular revival hymns reverberate down the valley to disturb Joe's conscience as he stares out into the darkness from the
hotel window at the very moment when Lottie and Ellen are sitting in the dark kitchen at home, united in despair. Joe in many
ways symbolizes the duality of man's nature—he is drawn to the
spiritual Hodgins as well as to the natural man Dan Higgins and
is "glad to be able to like them both." He wishes to be baptized
for his own peace of mind, but then wants things to remain "the
same as they've always been."

Irony plays over the entire narrative, including its title. Joe's
hypocritical and belated concern that Ellen go to church and be
"scared young" into respectability and his feeling of security at the
thought of her baptism are in ironical contrast with his own violation of her and his disapproval of her increasing religious serious-

ness. His confidence that their incident has passed without trouble is balanced by Lottie's happiness in him after he prays with her. Ellen's pathetic plight after a single misdemeanor is contrasted with the carefree attitude of Rose McIntyre who has been loose for years without paying any penalty or even offending religious people. But, as Joe meditates, a person "could go on doing anything he wanted to do in Eastmount, providing he had been doing it for some time." Public opinion and the conventional social code are similarly satirized. After the death of his wife and niece everybody in the village is "sorry for Joe, but evidently it hadn't done Ellen any good to go off to High School in the city and get in with older boys, and they remembered Ellen had been too lively at her age; her ultimate end seemed to be a vindication of established opinion in the village." Within days, however, Joe is regarded with suspicion and denounced as godless. His baptism regains for him public approval and even praise for "his depth of vision."

In its compression "An Autumn Penitent" is characteristic of Callaghan. The reader's sensorium for much of the action is Joe Harding. Through his perceptions minute details of description are realistically presented and an authentic rustic atmosphere created. When Ellen at the time of her unhappy confession becomes the sensorium, the style subtly changes to reflect her feeling of irresolution and hopelessness as well as her aunt's stunned acceptance of Joe's guilt. After Lottie's decision the two women's hesitancy is skilfully portrayed by the stops along the river, the strength of the wind opposing them and their difficulty in climbing up one of the bridge foundations from which to jump. The transition back to Joe's impressions is smoothly accomplished and the resolution of his own dilemma is consistent with his character and milieu.

III *"In His Own Country"*

The final part of *A Native Argosy* is also a novella, of one hundred and eight pages, entitled "In His Own Country." Originally published serially in the first three monthly issues of *Scribner's Magazine* in 1929, this story is set in the Georgian Bay town of Collingwood against a background of the Blue Mountain hills. Divided into eleven sections without subtitles, its action works out during a period of as many months the problem of a young newspaperman who proposes to reconcile science and religion for the twentieth century just as Thomas Aquinas "had taken the Artistotelian philosophy and learning of his time and rearranged it till it was acceptable to the church and a basis for a new Christian culture." Obviously unsuited by his ignorance of science and religion to tackle such a synthesis, he stubbornly persists, quits his job, loses his reputation, his wife's affection, and eventually his sanity. Ironically, it is his final stage of semi-paralysis and meaningless aphasia that brings to this frustrated prophet a belated honor "in his own country, and among his own kin, and in his own house."

Bill Lawson is portrayed as an average young man. Married for two years to a farmer's daughter, Flora, whom he had known throughout high school, he works for a semi-weekly paper, *The Standard*. Although in the words of his aged mother "Bill always did get impressions easy," he appears thoroughly stable: he waited until he "got enough money to build a house" before marrying; he ambitiously prefers the lower salary of the newspaper, which he expects someday to inherit from its owner, to the higher wages of the shipyard; he comes home happy from his work to romp with his dog, to play his mouth-organ for his wife, go swimming with her, follow the town sports or see movies.

Yet latent and catastrophic forces are suddenly triggered in this apparently normal and healthy personality on the very night before the narrative begins by the reading of an article on Thomas Aquinas. Bill's initial excitement, his growing preoccupation with his synthesis of all scientific knowledge, and his eventual obsession with his project to the exclusion of everyone and everything else are swiftly portrayed. Unable to talk over his ambition with anyone in his home town because he feels "few people would take it all in," he travels to Toronto to discuss his idea with the professors of St. Michael's College. In the city, however, after rehearsing several times the impressive story he will tell, he finds it strangely muddled. Distracted and ashamed, he convinces himself "it would be a waste of time talking to anybody while he was so unhappy," and returns home to finish his work entirely before consulting anyone about it. Bill's failure at this juncture to discuss rationally with some intelligent and sympathetic person who might have helped him regain a sense of perspective is crucial. But this failure only impels him to continue more determinedly. Neglecting his health and his wife, he investigates Roman Catholicism as the next logical step in his work. Its impact on his already overstrained mind is catalytic: he quits his job because of scruples of conscience about printing "lies and suggestions." His sanity finally snaps at the sight of his wife entertaining in their front room an old friend, Pete Hastings, and he flees in utter distraction. Discovered in Toronto in a state of emotional hysteria and confined for some time in an asylum, he is brought back home by his mother where as little more than a vegetable he becomes the wonder of the town.

The entire action and characterization are presented from the viewpoint of the protagonist's wife, Flora Lawson. A wholesome country girl in love with her husband and proud of his ambitions, she provides for the reader a sensitive record of her husband's deterioration and its emotional effect on her. Puzzled at first by his seriousness, she moves from sympathetic understanding through stages of growing concern, personal loneliness, fear, rejection, and ultimate reconciliation. Disenchanted with her solitary existence as Bill shuts himself up in his own strange land of books, she welcomes the companionship of a former friend, Pete Hastings, with his "handsome, generous way of making conversation." Following Bill's climactic discovery of Pete and her together, she withdraws to her parents' farm to sort out her feelings. Then restive, after Bill's return to town, she moves back into their home to care for him and find in the respect of society for him a sense of exhilaration and self-realization which compensates for her loss of his love. The varying and delicate responses of Flora to this bizzare situation are skilfully depicted. Her association of ideas and changing emotions, although indirectly expressed, are Joycean in their vividness:

At first she had been timid, like a little girl, now she breathed easily, ready to talk to him as though he were a child. "He knows I'm here, that's one thing he can't fool me about," she thought. She remembered that Gardner, the grocer, had insisted that Bill had many thoughts about people as he sat in the chair like a paralytic. Such a notion made her feel uncomfortable, and she moved away, afraid that he might be thinking of the night she had sat on the sofa in the front room with Pete Hastings. "Well, now, Bill," she said quietly and firmly, liking the sound of it, "well, now, Bill." That was the way she would have talked to him before he got sick and he would have listened good-naturedly. Now he remained aloof and solemn, his face white and thin, absolutely uninterested in her. She was impressed and knew she could not talk authoritatively. He was far beyond her, she could not touch him.[12]

Callaghan characteristically employs symbol and irony in working out the theme. The narrative opens with the repetition by Bill's mother of a family story:

Her grandmother, nervous and bewildered, had got off the boat just before it left the old land, and her husband hadn't missed her until they were a long way out. The poor woman had been terrified at the thought of going to a strange land, and so her husband had never heard of her again.

Like this ancestor, Bill becomes bewildered as he embarks for his strange land of metaphysics, his scholarly voyage is interrupted by madness, and he is never rationally heard from again. His wife Flora, already disillusioned with Bill's intellectual preoccupation, and yearning for physical companionship, reaffirms the earthy nature implied by her name in a symbolical baptism with dew: "She ran her fingers lightly along the surface of the grass, then touched her forehead with the moist tips. Three times she did it and her forehead felt cool."

The element of irony is strong, as the title suggests. That Bill with his inadequate education should even attempt to be a modern prophet is ironical, as are Flora's initial remarks about his aspiration: "I'll bet a dollar you'll get your name in the papers and the town'll do something about it later on." Bill does, indeed, become the town spectacle, "a great thinker and scholar" with "many wonderful things to tell some day." His long silence is broken first by a laugh and later by a pathetically mundane request, "I'd like a cream puff, or a chocolate eclair." Apart from the comic irony evident throughout, and especially marked in the concluding contentment of Flora, this remark, which is not funny to the person involved, provides virtually the only hint of overt humor in the entire narrative.

"In His Own Country" is a graphic psychological portrayal of a twentieth-century Don Quixote whose wits are permanently addled by reading science and religion rather than romances, and whose books and papers, like those of his more appealing predecessor, are cursed and burned. The focus in the second part of the story, as it was also in "An Autumn Penitent," is narrowed. Bill, since he ceases to be a rational human, does not continue to hold the reader's interest. After his return home as a mental patient, moreover, the narrative, although presented in a realistic and credible style, is lacking in dramatic incident and perhaps drawn out longer than the theme warrants.

The three sections of *A Native Argosy* present a cross-section of urban and rural life of ordinary North Americans during the late twenties. The grim effects of social deterioration and emotional isolation are portrayed in the careers of Callaghan's bewildered characters: suicide, jail, insanity, unemployment and disruption of familial and religious relations. The style, moreover, is appropriate to the cultural and psychological outlook of these misfits. Yet the total effect of the stories is to encourage the reader to be more tolerant, to enlarge his understanding of, and sympathy for, mankind beyond the bounds of conventional social and moral categories.

CHAPTER 3

That Summer in Paris

W HEN Callaghan left for Paris the day after he married Loretto Dee in April of 1929, his first two books had already
been published and his entree to the literary world assured. Stopping in New York en route, he and his bride were welcomed by
Max Perkins of Scribner's and entertained cordially by Sinclair
Lewis, who candidly remarked, "Do you know, Morley, Flaubert
would have liked your work." [1] On board ship the constant companion of the Callaghans was a Catholic chaplain for an American
penitentiary, who had walked to the execution chamber with sixteen men. This interesting conversationalist, who drank consider-
ably to alleviate intermittent attacks of fever, was to reappear in
different forms in subsequent novels of Callaghan.

Once in Paris, Callaghan soon began meeting the figures with
whom he had corresponded, who had published his stories, and
who were the leading writers of the day. In *That Summer in Paris*
(1963) he documents the experiences he had in that bright city of
the twenties, that "lighted place where the imagination was free."
His insight into the relationships among Robert McAlmon, Hemingway, Fitzgerald, James Joyce, Ford Madox Ford, other literary
exiles and himself is sensitive and refreshingly frank. The impact
of this colorful world on Callaghan is evident in the short stories
which he wrote in Paris as well as in the two larger works completed there, *It's Never Over* and *No Man's Meat*.

I *Bright City of the Twenties*

In Paris Callaghan first called on writer-publisher Robert McAlmon of Contact Press. As the latter belittled his erstwhile friend
Hemingway, Callaghan had his first demonstration abroad of the
petty jealousies and misunderstandings that existed in this hyper-
sensitive community. McAlmon's disturbing impression was soon

counterbalanced by Hemingway's call at Callaghan's hotel. The conversation of these two old Toronto friends turned to boxing and religion. Hemingway had recently become a Catholic and felt very good about it. Callaghan was not impressed:

But converts had always bored me. At that time in France there were many conversions among the intellectuals. Christian artists were finding new dignity and spiritual adventure in the neo-Thomism of Jacques Maritain. Most converts I had known had changed their faith but not their personalities or their temperaments. . . . My own problem was to relate a Christian enlightenment to some timeless process of becoming. A disgust with the flesh born of an alleged awareness of an approaching doomsday bored me, as did the flash of light that gave a man the arrogant assurance that he was the elect of God.[2]

Yet he recognized that Hemingway

was in fact intended to be a Mediterranean Catholic. And as it turned out, the older he got, the more often death kept hovering over his stories; he kept death in his work as a Medieval scholar might have kept a skull on his desk, to remind him of his last end.[3]

At this first reunion in Paris, Hemingway made it plain that even in such an activity as beer-drinking he was "the champ," and insisted that Callaghan demonstrate his ability in boxing.

After passing this crucial test Callaghan was invited by Hemingway to box weekly at the American Club. These bouts provide flashes of perception concerning the characters of both writers. Hemingway seemed to believe that his boxing was all important. On one occasion, when he was hit on the lip, he spat a mouthful of blood in Callaghan's face and solemnly offered as an apology, "That's what the bullfighters do when they're wounded. It's a way of showing contempt."[4] For what proved to be their final sparring session together their mutual friend Scott Fitzgerald acted as timekeeper. Watching with fascination he allowed the second round to go four minutes. It was to be an unhappy blunder: Hemingway, exasperated that he was not making a good showing in front of Fitzgerald, grew careless and was knocked flat on his back by Callaghan. Fitzgerald's impulsive admission of his mistake brought an angry retort from Hemingway and left a feeling of estrangement between the former friends.

Before this famous episode the Callaghans, with the assistance of two Montreal boys who were later to be fictionalized in "Now That April's Here," had found an apartment and had been introduced to other celebrated writers. On one memorable occasion McAlmon took them along for dinner with James Joyce and his wife Nora at the Trianon restaurant. Instead of the formidably unapproachable figure which Hemingway had intimated and the matronly Sylvia Beach so aggressively protected, the Callaghans found Joyce unpretentious and chatty. After dinner he invited the group back to his apartment for a drink. There, in lieu of the feast of literary opinions and elegant gossip which Callaghan had elatedly anticipated, he listened with impatience to a recital of McAlmon's reminiscences of a grandmother which Joyce interrupted by playing a delightfully suggestive record of an evangelical sermon by Aimee Semple McPherson.

Even more dramatic than the evening with the Joyces was the first introduction to Scott and Zelda Fitzgerald. Ringing the bell of their apartment one evening and receiving no answer, Callaghan and his wife were turning away in disappointment when the Fitzgeralds suddenly arrived home. They invited the Callaghans in for a visit. A discussion developed concerning a passage about courage in *A Farewell to Arms* over which Scott, who idolized Hemingway, was enthusiastic. Callaghan described it as "too deliberate. Maybe the rhythmic flow is too determined, and the passage emerges as a set piece." Zelda felt that the style sounded "pretty damned Biblical!" Apparently piqued that this Canadian was not suitably affected, Fitzgerald, with the unexpected preface "Would this impress you Morley?" attempted a headstand. Upset and somewhat humiliated by this antic, the Callaghans hurriedly withdrew. A couple of days later, however, the Fitzgeralds called and their friendliness and a subsequent dinner together charmed away this embarrassment.

Other Paris expatriates, although less legendary than McAlmon, Hemingway, Joyce and Fitzgerald, were equally colorful: Ford Madox Ford, with his searching pale-blue eyes and whispering voice; Ludwig Lewisohn, flushed with the success of his novel, *Mid-Channel* (1929); shrewd and cynical Michael Arlen, rich and famous after *The Green Hat* (1924); and Edward Titus, husband of Helena Rubinstein, book collector, publisher of the Black Manikin Press and editor of *This Quarter*, who generously loaned his apartment to the Callaghans during that August. In his observations on all these people Callaghan not only focuses on their literary abilities but also lights up with warm understanding their personal ambitions and inner tensions.

After the initial intoxication of Paris, "the great style centre of the twenties," Callaghan began working steadily on short stories for *The New Yorker* and on his novel, *It's Never Over*. As he remarks,

Paris streets were my workshop. While loafing along the streets ideas for the stories would grow in my head. Little street scenes would seem to distract me, would indeed get my full attention: the intent expression on the faces of men hurrying to the street urinals; workingmen quarreling under the eyes of a gendarme, each seeking the triumph of provoking the other to strike the first blow and get arrested.[5]

During these Paris walks he sought to express in his mind and later in his writings his impressions of life "freshly in a pattern that was a gay celebration of things as they were." With "a happy acceptance of reality" he aimed to

strip the language, and make the style, the method, all the psychological ramifications, the ambience of the relationships, all the one thing, so the reader couldn't make separations. Cezanne's apples. The appleness of apples. Yet just apples.[6]

As the autumn days became cooler the Callaghans grew restless to be home. After a final day with Hemingway at the Cathedral of Chartres they left Paris and returned via London and Dublin to Toronto. There Callaghan started on more short stories while he awaited the publication of the novel which he had completed in Paris.

II *It's Never Over* (1930)

In this novel, set in the Toronto of the late twenties, Callaghan's theme is the continuing and often tragic influence of past experience—war, love and friendship—on human lives. A wartime army captain, who has not been very successful in rehabilitating himself to civilian life, is hanged for the involuntary murder of a policeman who has treated him roughly in a speakeasy. The hanged man's sister, intent on possessing the lives of those who had been close to her brother so that they can never forget his death, deliberately involves them in her morbid obsession. Even her death cannot atone for the blighted lives left behind.

The story is presented through the central figure, John Hughes, talented bass soloist and close friend of the hanged man, Fred Thompson, as well as of his sister, Isabelle. The early chapters introduce the situation and through the hanging and funeral incidents develop the inextricable relationship of the past with the future. Isabelle refuses to accept the fact that her brother's death has a finality of its own, that life for the living must still go on normally. For her, "It's never over," since, as John reminds her, "you in your own thoughts are dodging in and out of the shadowy places and all the time it keeps getting darker in your own heart." [7] In the brief span between September and January these dark thoughts absorb not only John but his fiancée and accompanist, Lillian, who had known Fred briefly. They also envelop Ed Henley and Paul Ross, both former friends of Fred and admirers of Isabelle. These two interlocking triangles, complicated by the continuing impact of Fred's personality, dominate the novel and are emphasized right to its very end by the frequent repetition of the numeral three.

From the first page there is a constant reminder of this number. The streetcar stops three times on the evening before Fred's hanging as John is on his way to the Don Jail to join the crowd waiting for Fred's face to appear behind the three bars of the cell window. Three mounted policemen, three abrupt jerks of a bystander's jaw, three criminals with whom Father Mason had previously walked to the gallows, three drinks back in John's room, three people in the anteroom of the home where Fred's body lies, memories of three years ago, three late-blooming roses in the garden, three-storied houses, and three women in black at the cemetery all intensify the triangular relationships central to the plot.

By his use of description Callaghan keeps thoughts of death and decay constantly in the reader's mind. The novel appropriately begins in late September as the leaves are falling and ends with the "hard cold days of February" ahead. The Thompson garden shortly after Fred's funeral reflects the desolate aspects of this season:

Stems of flowers were still standing in the garden earth: withered flowers with broken stems; a few asters and zinnias still in bloom but fading in the daytime sun; tall stalks of flowers lying dry and dead against the fence. The leaves were still thick on the grapevine.[8]

In similar fashion the gloom of the winter twilight at the cemetery where Isabelle and Lillian kneel in the wet snow at Fred's grave is evocative of the depressing mood of the characters. The tall dark trees, the flock of small dark sparrows flitting across the gray sky and the heavy tombstone are effectively contrasted against the white snow. Yet the trickling water from the melting snow, like the thick grape leaves in Isabelle's garden, gives a sign of nature's underlying vitality.

Despite his early awareness of Isabelle's enveloping and malignant influence, John seems helpless to cope with her destructive power. Having persuaded Lillian to take an apartment in order to please John, Isabelle visits them and spoils their extramarital happiness together. She generates in Lillian's mind the notion that Lillian has really been in love with Fred. Then switching from the simple but genuine Ed Henley, Isabelle gives herself with abandon to Fred's wartime companion, Paul Ross. She deliberately draws the family priest, Father Mason, into her moral prostration by singling him out for confession. Her clandestine visit to John's room and his surrender to her strangely burning excitement lead to the eviction from his respectable boarding house and the loss of his position as church soloist. The discovery that she has admitted this indiscretion to Lillian and thus alienated her from him brings to a climax John's mounting resentment. His resolve to "rid himself of the source of all his unhappiness" is prevented only by Isabelle's impending death from pneumonia. Her funeral brings together the main characters and breaks permanently their relationship with each other.

As in *Strange Fugitive*, there are powerful naturalistic forces at work in *It's Never Over*. There is first a heritage of violence which is presented symbolically as reaching back to the jungle itself. In the opening scene, as Fred presses his face against the barred window of Don Jail to look at the curious crowd, the animals in Riverdale Zoo just across the river cry out as if in sympathetic protest against the legalized murder of capital punishment. Their cry is echoed by the prisoners who "always howled when one of them took the short walk to the gallows." Near the end of the narrative, as John stands outside Isabelle's house with murder in his heart, one of the sea lions from the nearby Zoo "cried out hoarsely."

Violence is the fatal flaw of Fred Thompson's character. "Violent, quick-tempered, and impulsive" by nature, at eighteen he made a bargain with an army recruiting sergeant to enlist "if he could punch him on the jaw first." As a young officer he once felt compelled to kill an old, gray-haired German prisoner who had gone berserk and was threatening to shoot Fred's own soldiers. The fatal quarrel with the policeman in a speakeasy is partly explained by his military training: "I've got a hunch that if he hadn't been at the war he wouldn't have hit that cop. The cop was hurting him and it seemed reasonable to kill him." [9] Recounting his friend's combat experience, Paul Ross himself relapses into a drunken hallucination of wartime danger and threatens to kill an imagined attacker. Violence is contagious, "a hanging draws everybody into it." It is not surprising that the vividness of this act, so constantly kept alive by Isabelle, should drive John Hughes in his exasperation to contemplate murder. Although ironically called by Lillian "the victim of . . . environment," John is presented in fact as ensnared in a web of experiences which are closely related with his environment. Unlike the hero of Thomas Wolfe's later novel, *The Web and the Rock* (1939), John has no father to whom to turn for strength and vision. He has, however, his own intelligence. He is no ignorant Harry Trotter. In addition to his extensive musical training, John reads widely: Synge's plays, and the Elizabethans, especially Marlowe. He is sophisticated and even tolerant in his view of music critics. He is perceptive in his early recognition of Isabelle's morbid intent. Yet he seems incapable of contending with her insidious attack.

Despite his ambition to be a great singer, he is as much one of the lost generation as his two veteran friends who cannot adjust to civilian life. As a paid soloist he has listened weekly to the empty moral sermons of the intolerant clergyman of St. Mark's Protestant Church. As a Roman Catholic who has not been to confession for about ten years he seeks guidance in vain from an old priest. Both representatives of the church only encourage John's determination to "restore his own feeling of decency and dignity" even though he should lose his soul. John's decision to murder Isabelle is worked out with a certain measure of objectivity:

It was, first of all, with him a matter of strong emotion, but just as essentially an ethical matter, for he was an educated man who had been taught for years that passions should be governed by reason; one ought to consider, then have a judgment and a conclusion, just as they used to in college in the first classes in logic.[10]

Although his head feels feverish, like Raskolnikov in Dostoevsky's *Crime and Punishment,* John deliberates carefully about whether "a man was ever entitled to take the life of another man who was a leech on society, sucking the blood out of people." [11] He tests this opinion on his rather commonplace landlady, Mrs. Stanley. At the very moment when he needs a disinterested opinion, she ironically supports his view with her own expressed desire to strangle the trollop who had run off with her second husband twenty-five years earlier.

The reminder, in the symbolical figure of the policeman ordering him to wait at a curb for the traffic signal, that he has neglected to consult his own security fails to deter John in his fixed purpose. The fulfilment of his plan, interrupted by Isabelle's admission of her imminent death, ironically would have put him in the same death cell as Fred, and would have bound him forever to that memory from which he was trying so desperately to escape. Fred's earlier physical death in accordance with the laws of society is symbolically paralleled by John's spiritual suicide in accordance with the doctrines of religion.

The deterioration of John's character is symbolized by the change in his material condition. He moves from the strait-laced Erringtons to Mrs. Stanley's cheap boarding house where the smell of gas pervades his room: "At first you could not smell it, and then once the odor was detected, you seemed to smell it all the time." Like the poison of Isabelle's obsession, the smell of gas grows increasingly stronger as the narrative progresses. It is only Isabelle's death that dispels the morbid atmosphere and lets in a fresh wind, anticipatory of spring, to awaken in afflicted spirits some healthy aspirations again: Lillian plans to return to giving piano lessons, and John to continue his operatic training in Italy. Amid the novel's corrosive events, Mrs. Thompson alone has the faith to absorb the shock of tragedy, even though the whole book seems to deny the comfort of that faith:

She would suffer bitterly, but always there was something to fall back on, for she was a good Catholic and believed that she, too, would soon die, and it would be only a little while before everything would be finally understood, and so sure was she of an inherent goodness in everybody, because of the compassion in her own nature, she thought death was often beautiful.[12]

It's Never Over, like *Strange Fugitive,* presents a realistic picture of the late twenties before the Wall Street crash. Hotel lobbies were still crowded, "everybody prosperous, many fat men stood there in fur coats and derby hats smoking cigars." [13] The Communist Party, represented by the revolutionary Gibbons, was involved in the dispute over left-wing and right-wing ideology and losing public support. Social democrats like Mr. Errington spoke ardently of political reform. Many wartime veterans like Paul Ross were increasingly disillusioned with their civil re-establishment. They recalled with grim humor the staged spectacle of recruiting rallies and recognized that there were no heroes in war, that "the trench is a gash, a wound" which sears men's souls. Although the events in the novel are less sensational than in *Strange Fugitive,* there is a sustained mood of excitement. This word "excitement," indeed, and its adjectival or verbal variants, is used so repeatedly as to become irritating. But it does heighten the intensity of suspense. The psychology is more subtle and complex than in the previous novel. Although Isabelle's motivation is not sufficiently analyzed and clarified, the characters generally are more aware of their problems, reflect more on events and the way in which human nature acts. Their dialogue is more natural, in that individual speeches are longer and less clipped than in *Strange Fugitive.* The description remains terse and simple. There is a skilful accumulation of apparently irrelevant detail which gradually builds up a distinct impression of the various characters as individuals. If the deliberately maintained evenness of tone becomes a disadvantage, the theme and its presentation continue to haunt the reader's imagination: the impact of the past, in this world at least, is never over!

III *No Man's Meat* (1931)

The sombre shades of *It's Never Over* are less typical of Paris than the mood that pervades *No Man's Meat*. Written rapidly for Edward W. Titus, whose apartment Callaghan and his wife occupied during August of 1929, this forty-two page novella was published in an autographed and numbered edition of five hundred and twenty-five copies by the Black Manikin Press in 1931. A clever *tour de force*, the story is notable for economy and artful humor.

Set in Echoe Lake, in that Algoma district of Northern Ontario which will figure so prominently in *A Broken Journey*, the action spans little more than twenty-four hours of an August day. There are only three main characters and they are all introduced in the first page. Bert Beddoes and his wife Teresa are waiting at their summer cottage for a visit from their old friend Jean Allen. The Beddoes in their marriage have long since "got beyond all undisciplined impulses and had achieved a contented peacefulness." Their childless life is orderly. Their daily routine is established and they enjoy "a steady reasoned happiness." Looking forward with anticipation to Jean's visit, they recall vaguely her recent travels and the fact that she had left her husband two years before.

From the moment of her arrival Jean, with her beauty, vitality and admiration for the country, excites her friends. In the sudden quiet after a gorgeous sunset she suggests a little gambling to pass the evening. She loses so consistently that Bert, in a final attempt to let her recoup her money, bets fifty dollars against her virtue. He wins, and Jean with the approval of Teresa insists on honoring the wager. The experience is traumatic. Jean becomes hysterical and Bert retires full of shame while his wife comforts their guest. Teresa returns briefly to his room with the revealing information that Jean had not left her husband to go away with another man

"but with a young woman she had met in another city. She loved
the young woman. Now she can hardly stand to be touched by a
man." After spending the night together, Jean and Teresa go away
together in the morning.

Bert Beddoes is the focal person through whose thoughts and
feelings this deft story with its surprising dénouement is unfolded.
He is introduced sitting up in bed looking out "over the dark lake
which was never blue from the cottage window in the morning
sun, even without a shadow from the big rock across the water."
His eager thoughts about Jean's adventurous life, his emotional
response to his wife and their tidy life together are swiftly delineated. "Dressed neatly in city clothes and shiny shoes," he goes
regularly for a morning walk, stopping to gossip with a neighbor-
ing farmer John Scott. Mrs. Scott, "full-throated and white-
breasted and black-haired," with her effortless movement "so
much a part of the untilled fields" outrages Beddoes' sense of order and dignity. His frank admiration of Jean's body as they relax
on the peak of the rock and his fear that her wild passion once
aroused might disturb him are developed with subtle irony. His
eager excitement concealed beneath his bland courtesy in the dice
game, his sincere desire to lose the crucial throw, paradoxically
and yet realistically combined with his powerful desire to sleep
with Jean, and his ironical sense of shame that "she was depressed
and terrified by a virginal shyness" are delicately conveyed. His
thought that "he had never seen a woman so aware that she had
been degraded and so ashamed of her own degradation" is con-
founded by his wife's revelation of Jean's homosexuality. After
this shock he reads the next morning "almost casually in Teresa's
handwriting, that she had never known how much she had loved
Jean and could not come back for a long time."

In retrospect the reader has little difficulty in recognizing the
aberration of Teresa and Jean. But the clues are artfully concealed. Teresa spends her mornings at the cottage woodcarving in
her workshop while her husband enjoys the traditionally feminine
gossip with the neighbour. Little gestures—her effort to make
everything she said sound "hard and practical," her warm embrace on Jean's arrival, the excitement with which she grips Bert's
hand as she watches Jean's Grecian dance and her sympathetic

response to Jean's hysteria—unobtrusively authenticate her final image. In the same way Jean's description is full of suggestiveness to the reader who looks back. Her Peter Pan hat, her love of Teresa's "bright metallic hardness," and her revulsion in the bedroom scene with Bert take on a completely different meaning in the light of Teresa's disclosure. Not only individually but also together these two kindred spirits are significantly described as part of an apparently conventional love triangle. As they go for a walk Bert follows "them with his eyes from the porch, the rounded full feminine figure and the thin nervous alert boy's body of his wife going together through the trees."

Apart from the characterization there are numerous images and symbols which subtly underline the homosexual aspects of the story. In the lake the great protruding rock which to Bert is "like an old woman leaning," has a different appearance for Teresa: "It's not like a woman at all. It's too hard and steady and urgent. I'm not sure it's like a man even. The time we paddled by the base in the shadow on the dark water and it hanging over us, it drove all the feelings out of me." Significantly Jean's response to this phallus-like symbol is identical: "the great rock looming overhead makes me feel a little nervous." Even more ironically evocative is the description of the ascent by Jean and Bert to the peak of the rock:

Steps lead up a path to the top of the rock but places were broken and they stopped at the entrance of a small grotto while he showed rough carvings made by Indians on the walls. "The Algonquins were here," he said, as they sat down in a small cleft, moss lined, between two jagged boulders. The sun was shining on them but they could not see the lake, and watching her stretching, relaxing, he wondered if she were having any of his thoughts. Under her skirts, pulled up carelessly above her knees, he saw faintly the whiteness of her thighs. Her eyes were closed. Beddoes had no thoughts at all. Though he did not want to make a mistake, the two of them were alone in the cleft in the rock and the feeling in her was not of the country at all. The beauty of her body, her exuberance and vivacity, was like the surface of the wild hard country; but the land was rocky and sterile underneath. He was ready to touch her tentatively when she opened her eyes and he knew she hadn't been thinking of him at all.

This passage includes two basic symbols which Callaghan develops throughout: the contrast of civilized and effete man with primitive and vital nature; and the contrast of surface beauty of landscape with barren unproductiveness of soil. As the peaceful Algonquins were driven out of the area by the savage Iroquois, so the rootless city folk with their decadent pleasures are spiritually rejected by the native farmers who are "part of the hard rocky soil." Jean's appearance and coloring reflect those of the country. Her red hat, dark hair ringed with grey and lively changes of expression match the brilliant hues, "the blending of all dark heavy oil primal colors" and changing moods of the lake and valley. Like its fields she too is sterile underneath. Ironically she is also like "the dark bluebottle green of first uncut pines" which Bert owns, and of which he declares, "they're not going to be cut."

Callaghan's remarkably sensuous and vivid description of the Algoma district illustrates his imaginative powers, for at the time he wrote the novella he had not visited this area. Jean and Teresa are the counterparts of Charles and Johnny in "Now That April's Here," and the inspiration for both stories came from the Paris café circle. Callaghan's happy choice of setting was actually dictated by the desire to place in a region which they had never visited a couple that was easily recognizable to the Left Bank group of 1929. This Canadian northland background contributes lyrical beauty, ironical overtones and even pathos to an otherwise sordid affair. The natural description delicately conveys the mixed feelings of Beddoes after the bedroom scene with Jean:

In his bedroom he was alone with his thoughts without any feeling of satisfaction, only uneasiness and restlessness. And he went to the window furthest from the lake, looking out at the path up the hill, trying to define straight elm trunks against the shadows on the hill. The smell of earth and of dead leaves came to him, and a wind getting stronger all the time blew over the hill, and on the other side of the house the water lapped sharply on the beach. There were no stars or lights in the land and looking out the lake window at the blackness of the water extending to the more impenetrable blackness of the rock's face in the night, was terrifying, for the skyline could not be seen from the window. Beddoes felt more uneasy, more confused than he had been in years, unable to regain the feeling of isolation.

That Summer in Paris

No Man's Meat, appropriately published in a limited edition, was obviously written for esoteric subscribers who would appreciate all its subtle nuances of irony and approve its suggestive symbolism. From the title's clever twist of Lucretius' familiar maxim ("One man's meat is another man's poison"), and the crude joke in "Meat," to the last paragraph, this sprightly novella is a masterful treatment, in technique and tone, of the Lesbian theme. Just as in *vers de société* tears lurk below the laughter, Callaghan's characteristic compassion for the helpless victim of life's vicissitudes underlies his surface effervescence. In its ending, when the story returns full cycle to a lonely contemplation of the lake country, the sensitive reader feels sympathetically the catastrophic changes which have taken place in Beddoes' life during a brief twenty-four hour period:

So accustomed was he to a steady calmness that he walked very slowly toward the cabin, shaking his head jerkily. The strong sun was shining brilliantly on the smooth lake, lighting up the desolate face of the big solid rock. Further around the lake the sun was just touching the top of the hill of the dark tall first growth pines, the best in the whole country.

CHAPTER 4

Changing Concepts

IN EARLIER narratives Callaghan had been dealing largely with characters who were ordinary people. Most of them never had the opportunity to develop intellectually or emotionally. Although portrayed with intuitive perception, their emotions are somewhat elementary. Even John Hughes in *It's Never Over*, despite his artistic talent and college education, is relatively immature; and the chief characters of *No Man's Meat*, though urbane and travelled, stand apart from the mainstream of life. In Callaghan's next three novels there is a distinct shift in both the type of characters presented and in the kind of theme treated. They reflect his increasingly variegated experience of life. To his intimate knowledge of limited aspects of the Canadian scene and to his sharp awareness of the continental sophistication of Paris were added in 1930 personal impressions of rural and urban life in the United States. During that year he spent eight months working in a secluded old farm house in Pennsylvania and making frequent trips to New York City to visit with literary friends and consult with editors of magazines who were publishing his stories.

I *A Broken Journey* (1932)

Beginning in Toronto and moving to the Algoma Hills on the north shore of Lake Superior, where Callaghan and his wife spent two weeks on a camping trip in 1930, *A Broken Journey* revolves around romantic love spoiled by misunderstanding, self-distrust and mutual lack of faith. Its two central figures are young and idealistic. Beautiful and intelligent Marion Gibbons, just returned from a trip out West, is inspired by the idea of going away to the north country for her honeymoon with Peter Gould. There at an old village, named Mission after the Michipicoten River on the banks of which it is situated, the lovers could really be together during the long days and nights. Peter eagerly responds to her suggestion. The only obstacle to their bright dream of happiness is Mrs. Gibbons, frustrated romantic turned sensualist, who has herself become possessively fond of Peter.

The three members of this triangle are swiftly delineated. Marion is full of childlike pleasure and warm sympathy with life. Elegant and poised she radiates an inner happiness, and appears to have resolved earlier doubts about herself, her mother and Peter:

After the university, when she was twenty-two, she had begun to think of her mother's life as something twisting and decaying at the very root within her till she had become a demoralized woman. She had thought also that a young woman ought to be able to do something with her own life, and a feeling which had been building up within her grew large and came to a peak one day, and she decided eagerly that if she lived alone, say in a religious order, she might find strength, intensity and courage. Though she wanted to keep a deep respect for her mother, she wanted at the same time to be utterly apart and different from her, clean, simple and untouched by any of the passions she felt had destroyed her mother. So she had become Sister Mary Rose, a simple person, in a world where there were many rich consolations.[1]

Marion's romantically idealistic nature, manifest in this brief attempt "to live in a world far beyond her mother's sensualism . . . to devote herself to the eternal Virgin that it might be a symbol for her life," also causes her later unhappiness. Confused and hurt by her mother's infatuation with Peter, Marion nobly renounces him. Though cool and quiet rather than boldly assertive, she reveals in this impulsively emotional decision that she has inherited many of her mother's traits.

Mrs. Gibbons, after twenty-three years of marriage, has a mixed reputation: some "thought her an unusually devout woman, and some thought her an old hussy beyond redemption." This same contradiction is apparent in her temperament:

As a girl she had been hot-tempered, bursting with vitality and eagerness and strong emotions that sometimes sent the blood rushing to her head and left her dizzy. For two years she had been a good, faithful wife to Gibbons, and after that, for twenty years or more, though they lived in the same house, they could not tolerate each other.[2]

During the war she drove a transport truck around the city and met a young, fair-haired officer.

To her he seemed so extraordinarily clean and his emotions were direct and honest. She thought of him all the time and prayed earnestly to express her thanks at being so happy. Her happiness seemed so fragile that she was always afraid of spoiling it, and besides, at this time she wanted to be a good woman, and used to think that in spite of the young officer's feelings, he would be happier if they could arrange a separation from her husband before they lived together. So she would not let him make love to her. All her nights were feverish with longing for him. She seemed to be actually afraid to let the young officer love her, as if afterward everything would be lost.

The officer's regiment left for France. A few months later he was killed. There had never been any kind of union between them. If she had only given herself to him she felt she might have been able to stand losing him. She thought herself the harshest, silliest woman in the world. She went twice to Europe as a sort of penitential pilgrimage; after that, when she decided she had no other loyalty, she wanted to have a great many lovers.[3]

For Mrs. Gibbons this young lover's image, which had been in her head for years, is renewed in Peter.

Peter Gould, "son of a retired country magistrate who had saved enough to send one son to college and to the law school," is a partial portrait of Callaghan himself. Of middle height, with large head, curly hair and blue eyes, Peter has been brought up by his parents on the poems of Edgar Allan Poe and libertarian passages from John Stuart Mill. Passionately in love with Marion, fond of Mrs. Gibbons with "her vivacious determination never to grow old," and mildly amused by her husband's ineffectually pompous denunciations of deteriorating political and economic conditions, Peter is presented as a happily exuberant young man. He is especially attached to his only brother Hubert, "a big, strong fellow who seemed to find a strange exultation and happiness in his own life." With Hubert, who had worked in northern lumber camps, mines and Western harvests, Peter enjoys an intimate relationship reminiscent of that of the two brothers in "Last Spring They Came Over."

Sullen from the disappointment of Marion's impulsive decision to leave him to her mother, Peter with almost implausible alacrity picks up a big, vulgar blonde, Patricia Lee, and moves into her hotel room. But this attempt to forget Marion is unsuccessful, and Pat, furious at his eventual rejection of her, pushes him down the stairs and severely injures his back. Marion, after narrowly escaping a casual intrigue herself and awakened by the recital of her mother's nostalgic longing for the wartime admirer, resolves to find Peter again. Although the two are reunited, their whole prospect has changed. Peter is so seriously incapacitated that he is virtually as dead for Marion as the young officer was for her mother. Their journey to Mission is a nightmare and once there Peter is forced to spend his entire time in bed. The lovers' dream of idyllic happiness is spoiled. Cheated of her anticipated happiness, Marion in frustrated despair surrenders her cherished virginity to the laconic guide, Steve.

A Broken Journey is infinitely more than the narrative of how a broken back ruins the resumption of an interrupted trip. It is a complex and subtle representation of the broken hopes and promises of life. Its presentation, although for the most part realistic, still has naturalistic elements. Marion feels herself a victim of heredity. Her longing for purity and attempt to escape her mother's sensualism are thwarted by untimely events. She succumbs not only to her own physical passion but symbolically to primordial Nature herself. As Hubert remarks, "A woman really wouldn't be having an affair with Steve at all. She would be having an affair with this country." [4] Like fish caught on a hook or the Indian boy who in trying to steal the loon's eggs was attacked and drowned,[5] both Marion and Peter are helpless to resist the vast, inexorable natural power of the north country.

Symbols abound in the story. The number three occurs repeatedly. Three oranges, three white-coated barbers, three pools, three fish, three jokes, three loons, three pails of blueberries and three final whistle blasts of the steamer all underline the interwoven triangular relationships: Peter, Marion, and Mrs. Gibbons; Peter, Marion and Patricia; Peter, Marion and Steve. Roses, too, have a special significance and symbolize love itself. As a novitiate Marion had taken the name Sister Mary Rose. This is her mother's favourite flower, which she allows no one else to plant or tend. Roses seem to represent Mrs. Gibbons' own aspirations, for when

Marion resolves to regain Peter she notices rosebushes in the garden where she had shared such eager hopes with him:

Red, white and yellow roses had bloomed and fallen a month ago, but yesterday, a white one, blooming later than the others, had blown and the white, withered petals in the clear night were splashed on the dark ground.[6]

There are symbolical foreshadowings of Marion's fall. For "a romantic poem that would be a symbol of North American experience" Peter conjures up an image of a

. . . bronzed woman standing on a hill looking out over a darkened field, listening for sounds from the battle: she heard the sound of flying hoofs, and the strange animal, the terrible horse, bearing a rider in shining armor, swept by, and she knew the field was soaked with the blood of her race. When the newcomers from the far-away world came rushing over the hill, she knew they would rape her, so she tried to send her soul after the horse, for it was so swift in its passing and its hoofbeats were still pounding in her ears.[7]

But the woman's face "always became Marion's face." Marion's sensual passion is like the dried punk which Steve taught her to ignite, Indian-fashion, by using a bow and sticks: "Once it gets lighted you can't put it out. It's always smouldering." [8] Although the flames which she later kindles on the beach arouse thoughts and emotions about Steve which glow and crackle, ironically she is unable in her demonstration of woodcraft to Peter to raise even a spark of fire.[9]

Characteristically, a spirit of irony informs the entire narrative. There is an obvious irony implicit in the saintly connotations of the chief characters' names. When Peter, although in physical agony, walks with Marion in a spirit of happy bravado to demonstrate how fit he is for the journey, they both giggle at the sight of a man walking with a cane. Just as ironically Marion and Hubert at Mission laugh at the Indians who hurry away to have a good laugh at them. In this escape to the rugged north country the thoughts and conversations of all three still return continually to the city.

There is the pervading irony of over-confidence which under the impact of misunderstanding and misfortune inevitably ends in broken faith. Again and again the lovers reaffirm their abiding and indestructible loyalty to each other. Despite constant reminders of the need for haste in seizing life's opportunities for happiness, Marion and Peter are forever missing them. As early as her first introduction of the idea of the trip he remarks: "Let us not waste a minute. I feel if we delay at all everything in the world will catch up to us." Her response is replete with Sophoclean irony: "What in the world could catch up to us? That country's so big and wild." [10] This note of the disregarded urgency of life continues throughout the novel. With her love for Peter reawakened by her mother's reminder of how quickly the years go, Marion feels, "When a thing's so close and you want it and you can reach out and touch it, you ought to be swift before you have a chance to cheat yourself." [11] Yet her reunion with Peter is delayed for that one day, crucial to their future, in which he is injured so critically that their life can never be the same. Even her surrender to Steve takes place just when Peter feels that he is recovering sufficiently to walk again soon.

The treatment of religion in this novel is penetratingly ironic. Father Vincent Sullivan, one of the three curates at the cathedral, prefigures Father Dowling of *Such Is My Beloved.* Young, good-natured and handsome with his white teeth, full red lips and straight black hair, he is full of zeal for his work. Yet his spiritual influence on the main characters is negligible. He is too timid to help Marion. When Peter, distressed in spirit over his relationship with Pat, says hello to him, Father Sullivan is so startled that he can only return the greeting gravely and pass by hurriedly on the other side of the road like the priest in the parable of the Good Samaritan. Even with Mrs. Gibbons, whom he respects for her elegance and dignity, he is ineffectual. In the face of her confession of past marital unhappiness he is flustered and ashamed. He withdraws "feeling that he had been close to something immensely ugly and evil that had nearly overwhelmed him." [12] The description of Father Sullivan's humiliating visit to Mrs. Gibbons is a vignette in its sympathetically satirical treatment of a young priest's inexperience and the fallibility of the Church's instrument.

This chapter, which is reminiscent of "A Predicament," is basically an expansion and modification of the short story entitled "The Young Priest" in *Now That April's Here*.

Less sympathetic is the satirical presentation of a young Anglican priest. Recently arrived in Northern Ontario from an English seminary, Mr. Richmond is an Anglo-Catholic who feels "that all Protestants are heretics." His pleasure at saying a mass for one of the Indian settlements and his enthusiastic conversation about High Church matters make his visits seem like "a kind of comic opera." [13]

In its comic undertone this scene resembles Marion's recollections of her brief sojourn in the convent, situated next door to Doctor Stanton's property:

Once the Mistress of the Novices had asked them all to pray that the doctor, who had declared definitely that his old home would never become a part of such an institution, might be persuaded to change his mind. God was often more willing to grant favors when the prayers came from fresh, eager young souls.[14]

The earnest prayers of the nuns for this event were apparently as unavailing as Marion's own private religious aspiration to emulate St. Teresa of Avila, "to lift herself into an ecstasy so she might see the image of Christ and feel Him beside her." [15] The image that materialized for her, however, was not Christ but ironically Christopher, a slender and romantic partner of college dances. Nor is Marion's mother more successful in her spiritual quest. What seems to Marion a "prayer of humble adoration" as her mother kneels with bowed head close by the altar of the Blessed Virgin is in reality as earth-bound as that of Hamlet's step-father.[16]

In this novel Callaghan has full scope for his descriptive powers. Marion's walk in the rain through the city streets, as she attempts to resolve her hurt bewilderment over her mother's affection for Peter, is vividly depicted. Especially striking are the sketches of evening coming on in the blue Algoma Hills, with their rocks and timber and vast expanses of water reflecting the darkening crimson sky. Such descriptions help to convey Marion's yearning for peace:

Night came on. A loon cried mournfully. The vast smooth water became slate gray, then the sky became slate gray, till the horizon faded
and there was no line between the sky and the water. All the rest of the
world seemed to have slipped down behind the vanishing skyline. . . .
It was like watching the night come on for the first time in a new
world. Then came one western shining star, then a handful of stars,
and the towering rocks on the shoreline loomed up dark and close till
they, too, were lost in the starlight. Only the great lapping lake waters
soothed the rugged shore. It was soon full night. As the northern lights
began to sweep vastly across the sky, she felt a strange harmony and
peace all around her, and she felt herself groping toward it and trying
to become a part of it. She felt, as her heart began to beat heavily, that
her love for Peter was the way toward a more complete and final peace
than any she had ever known, and that they might both know the
mystery that rounded out the night.[17]

Such idyllic passages may arouse in the reader hope for a happy
outcome. But the writer's artistic integrity constantly brings the
recurring mood of eagerness back to reality. For Callaghan's
power of minute observation is equally evident in the sordid aspects of life. In a letter to him dated November 16, 1931, on this
very subject, Max Perkins of Scribner's felt that many of the mean
details presented in *A Broken Journey* were "not compatible with
the glamour of this romance, or its tragical conclusion":

For instance, I think that perhaps the whole physical element of love is
over-emphasized. Now, Peter takes up with the other girl only because
he considers his love-affair with Marion has concluded, and perhaps
too much is made of his relations with the other girl, and he treats her
too brutally at the end. Because this story is about the love between
Marion and Peter, and it is a different kind of love from the merely
physical, and should be so presented. And in the end of the story,
where the idyllic qualities are more than ever marked, I do not think
that the affair with the guide need be gone into to the degree that it is.
The only important thing about it is that it happened, and in circumstances which make it seem inevitable and excusable. In many places
through the story there are almost naturalistic details, which do not
seem to me to blend with the story's intent and motive. I would even
question the incident of the false teeth. That was so horrible and unpleasant, and yet I recognize that it had a great value too.[18]

In making these remarks Perkins admitted that he was not sure if he was too much influenced by literary conventions. Yet Callaghan apparently took note of the criticism, for in the novels which immediately followed *A Broken Journey* he was successful in selecting details appropriate to his themes.

II *Such Is My Beloved* (1934)

In short stories Callaghan had overtly treated issues that confront Roman Catholics and had dealt with them as an integral part of *It's Never Over* and *A Broken Journey. Such Is My Beloved,* the first and only novel in which he turns to an elaborate treatment of a religious theme, was for him simply the pursuit of a congenial subject. Unlike François Mauriac, who was born a Catholic, or Graham Greene, who became an intellectual convert, Callaghan was not giving expression to an experience of religious crisis or conversion. There was no incompatible clash between the claims of the body and those of the soul, between nature and grace, tormenting him. He had been born and brought up in a liberal Catholic tradition, educated in public primary and secondary schools, and introduced in college to Thomist philosophy. Individualistic and independent in his intellectual outlook, he treated metaphysics "with grudging suspicion. . . . Nothing could be taken on authority. . . . Orthodoxy was for fat comfortable inert people who agreed to pretend." [19] Callaghan, although he probed its deficiencies, did not reject his religious heritage and was never one of the lost generation in the sense of feeling that all the gods were dead. The Catholic thought, tradition and symbol with which he was imbued provided a natural standard not only for assessing himself but also for creating characters and situations, regardless of whether religious issues were openly involved. An extrovert by nature, moreover, he had no sense of social alienation.

In *Such Is My Beloved* Callaghan views life in a specifically Roman Catholic rather than a generically Christian context. At the particular time he was writing this novel he was enjoying an association with the noted neo-Thomist philosopher Jacques Maritain, who was visiting lecturer at the Institute of Medieval Studies of St. Michael's College. To Maritain, indeed, the book is dedicated: "To Those Times With M. In The Winter of 1933." Using traditional symbolism Callaghan depicts an irreligious world of cynicism and pessimism, of betrayal and frustrated justice. Yet in this fallen world with its failure of human love there is also a reminder of that divine love which can alter the apparently fatalistic destiny of ordinary mortals.

Set in a large industrial city, which although not mentioned by name is recognizably Toronto again, the action of *Such Is My Beloved* begins in February and ends shortly after Easter. Its general theme is enunciated in the epigraph, taken from the Song of Solomon (VIII.7): "Many waters can not quench love, neither can the floods drown it. If a man would give all the substance of his house for love, it would utterly be contemned." The story is concerned with the attempt of a young priest to redeem two prostitutes, his apparent failure in the face of social opposition and hierarchical disapproval, his profound disappointment and eventual commitment to an asylum. Although the narrative element is thin and the characters are few, the book is rich in symbol and irony.

Introduced as "the most eager young priest at the Cathedral," Father Stephen Dowling is the dominating figure of the novel:

From the time of his ordination he had approached every bit of parish work with enthusiasm and preached with such passion that old Father Anglin, the pastor at the Cathedral, used to shake his head and wonder if the bishop could be advised to send him to some quiet country town where he would not have to worry about so many controversial problems. It was rather disturbing for the older priest and some of the old and prosperous parishioners, too, to have a young man around who was apt to attack any difficult social problem with all the intensity of his very ardent nature. Last Sunday, for instance, at the ten o'clock mass, Father Dowling had preached a sermon on the inevitable separation between Christianity and the bourgeois world, and he spoke with a fierce warm conviction, standing in the pulpit and shaking his fist while his smooth black hair waved back from his wide white forehead and his cheeks were flushed from his glowing enthusiasm.[20]

With all this zeal he has a warm personality and a charming smile that makes all those with whom he associates feel amiable and even jolly. Returning one evening from reassuring old Mrs. Schwartz that she would not die, and with his head full of thoughts for a bold sermon "on the building of a society on Christian principles," he is accosted by two prostitutes. Fleeing at first in embarrassment, he returns quickly, to help them. Unlike Father Francis in "A Predicament," Father Dowling does not evade his duty as a priest. On the street corner, however, with his muffler concealing his clerical collar, he fails to impress the girls with his serious purpose.

From this initial meeting Father Dowling feels within himself a compassion growing "so intense it must surely partake of the nature of divine love." [21] With the end of the first chapter, then, the religious symbolism is already clearly emerging. The novel's title echoes the words from Heaven on the occasion of Jesus' baptism by John the Baptist. Father Dowling's love for these wretched souls is Christ-like: it transcends human conventions and yet must work within them. Inside the cheap Standard Hotel, before the girls' faded grey-white door which suggests sullied purity, he stands and knocks. Admitted, he somehow touches Ronnie and Midge with his genial radiance. But his mission to rehabilitate them is misunderstood or opposed by society and the Church. He cannot confide in his fellow priests at the Cathedral: neither young Father Jolly, with his good-natured malice and complacent enjoyment of comfortable living, nor old Father Anglin with his lack of faith in social progress, can comprehend. Turning hopefully among the parishioners to wealthy lawyer James Robison and his wife for help, Father Dowling meets with regretful sympathy and pious cruelty. To them the possibility of a scandal, or worse, of being made to appear foolish, makes inevitable the necessity of reporting the priest to his bishop.

Just as Robison in denying his pastor and—at the insistence of Mrs. Robison—in betraying Dowling is symbolic of the disciples Peter and Judas Iscariot, so also is Bishop Foley symbolical of Pontius Pilate. He is a man of conscience, sincere in his devotion to the Church but with "a fine mind for politics, an intuition that compelled him to do the expedient thing." [22] As he hears Robison's story the bishop is less anxious about the priest's behaviour than about the possible effect that any public scandal may have on a charity campaign soon to be launched in the city. Later, hearing Father Dowling's side, the bishop is not unsympathetic: "One part of his mind was telling him that the young priest was utterly without blame; the other part of his mind was urging him to be rational, to be firm, to administer his office according to his highest conception of duty." [23] His discreet suggestion to the lawyer that they pray for the police to "arrest the girls and get them out of the way" is understandable enough; but it is as ironic as his pharisaical concern for public charity and cynical prohibition of Father Dowling's private charity.

Veronica (Ronnie) Olsen and Catherine (Midge) Bourassa suggest the Biblical woman taken in adultery. A native of Detroit, Ronnie came from a broken home: her divorced parents "just used her as a means of hurting each other." [24] At the first opportunity she left them for a job in a department store. But as the depression deepened, her working hours grew shorter. To pay her room rent she began accepting gifts from men, and when she lost her job became an outright prostitute. Her companion Midge was the oldest girl in a large French-Canadian family of Montreal. Excited by the bustle of the St. Lawrence waterfront, she left Montreal with a lover called Andy who soon abandoned her to a host of nameless paramours. Petite, voluptuous and warmly impulsive, in contrast with tall, angular and brooding Ronnie, Midge suffers the additional humiliation of an unwelcome pregnancy.

The agency of Satan is symbolized in the roles of the procurer and the keeper of the bawdy house. Ronnie's lover, Lou Wilenski, is a cheap and arrogant hoodlum. He is the natural antagonist of Father Dowling. But in the latter's presence his intended sarcasm is disarmed and he is powerless against the influence of the priest. Despite his depravity, however, Lou is also touched by love. He feels tenderly towards Ronnie to whom he represents the essence of kindness because he appreciates her good qualities. Completely untouched by any such element of goodness, Henry C. Baer, proprietor of the Standard Hotel, is fat and cynical. His sneering thoughts about Father Dowling's visits to the hotel are ironical and grimly humorous: "There goes the lamb of God again. I wonder which one he likes." [25] As Baer remarks to Lou, "It's all the same to me whether they take a rabbit or a priest or a czar of Russia up there, as long as they make it pay." [26]

The response of society throughout the ages to people like Father Dowling, who put into practice a concept that in theory is unassailable, has been consistent. Shaw in his Preface to *Saint*

Joan remarks, "the strange superiority of Christ and the fear it inspires elicit a shriek of Crucify Him from all who cannot divine its benevolence. Socrates has to drink the hemlock, Christ to hang on the cross, and Joan to burn at the stake." The Robisons, and in particular Mrs. Robison, feel the intolerable humiliation of being exposed as less sincere than Father Dowling. When he bears only good will he arouses in their hearts fear and distrust. His indignation at Mrs. Robison's cold reception of the prostitutes implies "a contemptuous criticism of her manner of living and her spiritual and social life, and the more she pondered, the more she felt with deep sincerity that he was misguided, and the more she was determined to cling desperately to her faith in her own wisdom." [27] In her worldly twentieth-century wisdom she sees the problem from a sociological rather than a Christian point of view: "all prostitutes are feeble-minded." Ironically juxtaposed against this comment are Father Dowling's angry and disgusted thoughts back in his own room:

Mary Magdalen was feeble-minded and Mary of Egypt, too, and Joan of Arc heard voices; it becomes simply a problem of breeding, once you can sterilize the unfit it's easy to breed the whores out of existence, and the mentally fit are always moral, and immorality is simple feeble-mindedness.[28]

Another modern and equally impersonal remedy for the situation confronting Ronnie and Midge is economic, that of social revolution. This is the solution offered by Father Dowling's good friend Charlie Stewart, a medical student, who is a passionate Marxist. Good-natured, perceptive "and above all, a man with a simple heart," his practical concern for the poor and oppressed is an ironic judgment on the bishop's orthodox expediency. But Charlie is still only a healer of bodies. He disagrees with Father Dowling's attitude toward the girls:

In the perfectly organized state there would be no street walkers. If the state has a proper control of the means of production and the means of livelihood, it's never necessary for a woman to go on the streets. No woman of her own accord would ever do such work. It's too damned hard. But if in the ideal state there were still women who were street walkers out of laziness or a refusal to work steadily then they would be kicked out or interned somewhere for laziness, or as non-producers. Then they'd have to work or starve. Your mistake is seeing this as a religious problem. It's really an economic problem.[29]

In this presentation .of divine love struggling to make itself manifest within a human framework, where the gift of freedom of choice paradoxically thwarts divine purpose, Callaghan's symbolism and irony engross the reader's imagination. The names of the chief characters, Stephen (the first Christian martyr), Veronica (who gave her kerchief to Christ to wipe the perspiration from his face) and Catherine (a virgin martyr), evoke religious overtones in the reader's mind. Professor Malcolm Ross, in his Introduction to the "New Canadian Library" edition of *Such Is My Beloved,* analyzes the "threefold (yet unitary) set of symbols" which Callaghan employs in treating his theme:

Each of Callaghan's key symbols is a realization, in its own degree, of the Body of Christ, and each is held by its opposite (its negation) in a perpetual tension, the tension of irony. (1) The Church is the Mystical Body of Christ, yet the Church is necessarily inserted in time and composed of that very dust which must to dust return—i.e. the Church is divine; the Church is a human institution. (2) The flesh, the rapturous, sensual flesh of the Song of Songs, adorns the Church as the Bride of Christ. The Church is raised from the dust, redeemed from time in the heavenly marriage: yet this is that selfsame flesh which wars with the spirit, Satan's snare, the symbol of sin and sickness and death. (3) The Sacrifice, the Body as given on the Cross, the sacrament of the altar, the life-giving death which the Church celebrates (and in which it participates) is the ultimate act by which the fallen world is redeemed—its wounds bound up: yet two pathetic girls, victims (and symbols) of the world's sin, are sacrificed, and by a prelate of the Church, to the world's hypocrisy. And a broken priest is exiled from the altar and the joy of his youth.

Since the conclusion of the action takes place at Easter time, the symbolical significance of events gives an additional meaning to the drama. Father Dowling's first meal with the girls is in their own "upper room" of the hotel, and the cheap red wine and sandwiches wrapped in a white napkin are the elements of their last supper together. The girls, like the two thieves crucified with Christ, somehow share Father Dowling's sacrificial punishment.

Like Christ, Father Dowling has his moment of despair when he believes himself forsaken. Yet in the final lines of the book, content in his moments of clarity to continue a commentary on the Song of Songs, he is seen against the background of an evening sky in which the three theological virtues of faith, hope and charity shine as brightly as in Dante's *Divine Comedy:*

There was a peace within him as he watched the calm, eternal water swelling darkly against the one faint streak of light, the cold night light on the skyline. High in the sky three stars were out. His love seemed suddenly to be as steadfast as those stars, as wide as the water, and still flowing within him like the cold smooth waves still rolling on the shore.

Absorbing as is the working out of these symbols, the most moving quality in the novel is the characterization of Father Dowling. He is the central figure who evokes both an imaginative and an emotional response in the reader. For Father Dowling is captivatingly human. To the sophisticated—the prostitutes, the Robisons, the bishop, Charlie Stewart, and often to the reader—Father Dowling is naïve: he means well but he just doesn't realize the facts of life. And yet he has a warmly compassionate understanding of the needs of humanity. He knows that "it's hard to be hungry and be a Christian." He is not immune to carnal temptation, but he faces his one moment of passionate impulse, overcomes without shame and is strengthened by this moral victory. He compromises in his attitude to the mixed marriage proposed between Charlie Stewart and Pauline, and can sympathize with the despair with which the Cinzanos, burdened by twelve children, view the Church's doctrine of birth control. He even tells a white lie, claiming that Ronnie and Midge are his nieces, so that Pauline will buy them clothes, which ironically are used to make them more attractive as street-walkers. He neglects sending money to his mother in order to spend it on the girls. When Mrs. Schwartz eventually dies in peace, Father Dowling reflects how much more the living need the peace and justice of God than the souls of such dead. As he reads the news of the day, his heart reaches out to "all those restless souls who were struggling and dying all over without consolation":

. . . two young men had held up a girl and robbed her of her purse. A young mother had tried to kill herself and her child because they were without food and a place to live. This spring there were floods in China and talk of war all over Europe, and there were riots in Germany and a hunger march on London. It was the same all over. In Canada one-third of the workers had no jobs.[30]

Through his response to the dilemma of the girls Father Dowling gains a new concept of Christianity which rises above all the dogmas of orthodoxy: "That desire to make each moment precious, to make the immediate eternal, or rather to see the eternal in the immediate." [31] Thus he rebukes the bishop, who wonders how successful the attempt to reclaim the prostitutes has been, with the comment, "Even a dream of social betterment usually is a bitter disappointment. We've got to accept the disappointment and go on. All of us must be terribly disappointing to God. By any standard of justice God might have abandoned us all long ago." [32] This gentle and humble affirmation of his faith in the destiny of individual man is affecting in its unequivocal simplicity.

Father Dowling's final lapse into intermittent insanity is caused by his worry over Ronnie and Midge. The world's hypocrisy has interrupted his reflection in their lives of that radiance of divine love which he himself has experienced. His end is consistent with literary myth. Swift's Gulliver, after his glimpse of "the perfection of nature" as revealed in the Houyhnhnms, reacts so eccentrically to his fellow humans that he is considered deranged. An even more apt parallel exists in the seventh book of Plato's *Republic* where Socrates relates to Glaucon in the simile of the cave how one of the prisoners is brought up into the sunlight. When he has become accustomed to the brightness he feels sorry for those still down in the shadows. Taken back to the cave, he is blinded by the darkness, appears awkward and excites ridicule among his companions. But in time his glimpse of the absolute form of the Good helps him to comprehend more fully its shadowy images manifest to the unenlightened.

Despite the complex symbolism and elaborate irony of *Such Is My Beloved*, Callaghan's style is itself straightforward and simple. Although most of the book is presented through the focus of Father Dowling, incisive glimpses are given into the thought processes of all the main characters. The often child-like language of

Father Dowling realistically reflects his own directness, awkward embarrassment or unrestrained and boyish pleasure. Robison is as legalistically guarded in his remarks as the bishop is aloof and discreet. The dialogue in the circle of friends around Midge and Ronnie demonstrates again Callaghan's command of the language of the street. Equally realistic are his descriptive passages. The cheap hotel room of the prostitutes, with its faded wall-paper and curtains and its threadbare carpet, is in marked contrast to the gracious drawing room of the Robison home with its splendid furniture and rugs. The street scenes portrayed in the various conditions of winter and spring evocatively reflect the mood of the action. When, for example, Father Dowling after learning that the girls have been arrested leaves the Standard Hotel for the last time, he is wondering what will become of them. As he looks up and down the streeet a "little piece of paper by the curb, caught in a gust of wind, went spinning and eddying along the road till it was out of sight." [33] Thus Callaghan's descriptive image suggests not only the fate of Ronnie and Midge but also the plight of society itself during the bleak Depression period.

Such Is My Beloved, the last of Callaghan's novels to be published by Scribner's, has an appeal that is timeless. Callaghan captures what Henry James calls "the strange irregular rhythm of life" in this moving representation of the tragic duality of man, creature of doubt and denial but also of restless and persistent urge towards something yet unattained. The gulf between aspirations and actions, between the ideal and actuality, is powerfully delineated in Father Dowling and his relationships with others. In his early works, although never a naturalistic writer, Callaghan had shown man as almost at the mercy of heredity, social pressures, and his own passions. In this novel there is an increasing emphasis on the importance of the individual's freedom of choice and on moral judgment. Despite repeated reversals, Father Dowling penetrates beyond the "Chaos of Thought and Passion, all confused" which characterizes the human condition to a calm faith in God's continuing concern for man.

III   *They Shall Inherit The Earth* (1935)

Like his previous novel, *They Shall Inherit The Earth* also echoes a biblical phrase in its title, develops the motifs of love and justice, and characteristically includes religious symbolism. More penetrating in its psychological analysis of the interaction between personalities than any of his previous work, this novel marks a new level of complexity and variety in its structure and characterization. Even the setting is multiple and includes city, lake country and northern wilderness.

The action of *They Shall Inherit The Earth* is simple and straight-forward. Andrew Aikenhead persuades his son Michael after years of hostile separation to come for a week to the family lakeside home. There Andrew's second wife Marthe, her son Dave Choate, Michael, his sister Sheila and her fiancé Dr. Ross Hillquist, son of Andrew's partner, gather. Angered by the designs of Dave on Sheila and his assertion that the first Mrs. Aikenhead had been insane, Michael badgers his step-brother into diving from a boat, jabs him with an oar, harasses his attempts to swim to shore, and then ignores his drowning cries for help. When Dave's bruised body is discovered, Michael denies any knowledge of the death and allows the suspicion of murder to fall upon his father. Tormented for months by his sense of guilt, Michael eventually discovers in the love of Anna Prychoda a healing influence which leads him to confess to, and become reconciled with, his father.

The religious symbolism is threefold. From the outset the parallel of the prodigal son (Luke XV. 11-24) is suggested. Michael, an unemployed graduate civil engineer, "had left his father's house when he started at the university." He is spending his meager funds in the riotous living of taverns, associating with such disreputable characters as Huck Farr in whose company he recalls "the names of all the little chippies he had ever known." [34] He falls upon a time of great famine and is himself in want. His proposed return to the family's country home is eagerly anticipated by his father. At the lake Michael is greeted by his step-brother, "Welcome the prodigal, the lost one has returned." [35] Filled with thoughts of how often he has wakened in the night "full of remorse at the separation between him and his people," Michael, along with Ross Hillquist, approaches the old stone house of his youth where his father Andrew is waiting. "When they were still some distance off, he left his wife and Sheila and Jay Hillquist who had come out to stand beside him, and he rushed down the path to join his son." [36] This reunion, however, because of Dave's drowning, leads only to a more serious estrangement. On one occasion during this period Mike thinks bitterly "of his father's house, and his father's friends and their land of plenty." [37] The final reconciliation of father and son occurs only in the last pages of the book, when Michael comes in sorrow and shame to beg forgiveness for allowing the blame of Dave's death to fall on his father. And Andrew responds eagerly to this reunion with his lost son.

The story of Cain and Abel (Genesis II. 1-17) also underlies Michael's ordeal. He is angry because of the contrast between his own hard existence and his step-brother's life of luxury. His responsibility for Dave's drowning makes Michael spiritually like Cain, "a fugitive and a wanderer on the earth." During Anna's pregnancy the parents suggestively refer to the unborn baby as "Abe." Yet only as he faces in the hospital the possibility of Anna's death in childbirth does Michael admit the enormity of his crime and remorsefully mumble to himself: "I'm sorry, Dave. I know how you wanted to live. I know how wonderful it is just to go on living." [38] In these anguished moments he realizes, as his name in Hebrew signifies, that he is "like unto the Lord." He has taken life and he is giving life. In the birth of his son and his own paternal love Michael discovers a love for his father and begins a regeneration. He apologizes to Andrew "timidly, like a child," and this humility and repentance eventually bring him peace of mind.

The title itself suggests another biblical symbol that is developed. This motif, taken from the beatitudes of the Sermon on the Mount (Matthew V. 5), is particularly exemplified in the character of Anna Prychoda, whose name in the Hebrew form Hannah signifies "grace." As Michael lies awake in "the dark night world of his despair" and thinks of all the restless souls like himself he looks wonderingly at Anna sleeping peacefully beside him:

"She's everything I'm not," he thought. She went on from day to day, living and loving and exposing the fullness and wholeness of herself to the life around her. If to be poor in spirit meant to be without false pride, to be humble enough to forget oneself, then she was poor in spirit, for she gave herself to everything that touched her, she let herself be, she lost herself in the fullness of the world, and in losing herself she found the world, and she possessed her own soul. People like her could have everything. They could inherit the earth.[39]

Throughout the novel Michael is preoccupied with the operation of justice, both human and divine, in this world. Professor
Frank Watt in his Introduction to the "New Canadian Library"
edition of *They Shall Inherit The Earth* comments:

Michael's search for self-justification—for justice—has three aspects:
the social or political, the personal or religious, and the natural; and
three main settings are used to develop it, appropriate to Michael as a
social being (the city), as a person (his once-paradisal family home in
the country), and as a natural creature (the wilderness of the wolf-
hunt). In the city Michael eventually rejects the social panacea of
communism as irrelevant to his essential personal condition; in his family relations he realizes at last that a hard-hearted individualistic aloof-
ness is untenable; and in the wilderness he sees a metaphysic of natural
harmony in which slayer and slain each have a part, but which is a
pattern of justice offering small consolation to the individual.

Each of these three aspects of justice is concretely symbolized.
Although the fact "that he should be free and his father should
be bearing the blame for Dave Choate's death" does not seem
unjust to him, Michael experiences "a great hunger to find that
there could be justice among human beings on earth." [40] The discontented faces of unemployed, the long lines outside the soup
kitchens, the evictions of families of men unable to find work, the
brutal crimes and vicious punishments all seem a mockery of order and justice. As a remedy for this social disorder the appeal of
communism is presented by the characters of William Johnson
and his ardent wife. Listening to him "proclaiming that a human
being could find dignity carrying on the struggle of all the humble
people who ever lived on the earth," Michael "himself, began to
feel humble, and he longed to free himself from his distress by
losing himself in his friend's disinterested hope for the poor of the
world." [41] Looked at from the socialist point of view the loss of
Dave's "useless, parasitical life" is economically unimportant. And
Anna's predicament, in which she seems about to surrender to
Huck Farr "because she's broke and sort of punch drunk from
being pushed around," is to Johnson "a perfect example of economic necessity." [42] This rejection of Anna as an individual is un-
acceptable to Michael. Even though he senses in Anna's father a
less impersonal kind of communism and feels close to him, Mi-

chael realizes that such a revolution will not bring in the millennium. As he remarks to Johnson, "You seem to think that you just have to have an economic house cleaning and we'll all get justice. None of us will get justice, personal justice, and we'll start hungering for it all over again." [43]

In his experience of wolf-hunting in the semi-wilderness of the Georgian Bay district with Ross Hillquist and an Indian guide named Jo, Michael sees another aspect of justice. Initially he feels that in this setting he could lose his dreadful fear and "just be an organism, part of the living things around." [44] He believes that the wolf is an individual and kills from the sheer lust of killing. Like his cynical friend, Huck Farr, with his hard eyes and predatory instinct for women, it "was beyond any moral law or loathing." [45]

"Any enemy of the race you call a wolf because he knows no moral law, and that's why you can't organize society, because it's full of wolves, and they don't know justice, and don't want it. The financial brigands and labor exploiters and the war profiteers and the Wall Street sharks and nearly anybody who tries to put his head up in a world of private profit, what are they? Wolves I tell you." [46]

At first this protest against the confusion of his own life seems to be borne out by the action of the wolves, who are seen on the ridge as three mysterious specks moving round and round in a kind of primitive ritual and then disappearing. That night as he listens to "the threatening wolf's moan out of the night and the snow, deeper even than that, out of the core of the hostile world," [47] the only comfort he finds in his anguished soul is the love he shares with Anna on whose name he calls. The following day when their apparent wanton slaughter of deer is discovered, Michael savagely remarks, "useless, purposeless, wanton slaughter. You had the nerve to talk to me last night about meaning and order in life and justice and God knows what else, Ross. Look at it. Put your nose down and try and smell it. The natural history of natural justice." [48] Indian Jo refutes this outburst by his explanation of how this meat is simply in cold storage for the she-wolf when she whelps and is unable to leave her litter to forage.

As they return from the hunt Michael ponders about this natural justice:

"Is it justice for the wolves when the deer are slain? Is it justice for the deer to wait and be slain, and can they cry out and complain, and who would hear that cry and know what it meant? My own conception of justice spares me and kills my father. Day after day I try to balance the book so I will be justified. The old Greeks talked a lot about justice. Socrates. The giving of every man his due. What is any man entitled to?" [49]

Confused in his attempt to understand the working out of the pattern of justice he exclaims:

"But what about justice for each single human being? That must be there too. I stink with pride when I judge my father's life, or Dave Choate's life." And as he walked on, closing his eyes against the biting snow, he became very humble, and he thought, "I know everything will have some meaning if I stop passing judgment on other people, and forget about myself, and let myself look at the world with whatever goodness there is in me." [50]

If this justice of nature offers little consolation for the individual human, there is yet another concept to be found in religion. This aspect is presented through the character of Nathaniel Benjamin, a Jew converted to Christianity and therefore symbolic of the entire Judaeo-Christian tradition. Initially Michael resents Benjamin's sympathetic feeling:

"The trouble with Christians like you is that you're never happy unless you have someone to pity. You want to be surrounded by wretched people so you can exhibit in full swing the tenderness in your nature and the love you think you ought to have for people. There's no use talking about the way I feel about that drowning with a guy like you because you wouldn't understand it. You're a guy who believes in free will and the responsibility of the individual soul, and the soul's destiny." [51]

Eventually, however, he comes to appreciate the tenderness of Benjamin, torn between "Jewish arrogance" and "Christian humility." Realizing the pride of his own intellectual assumptions and accepting what he has done, Michael finally cries out in anguish: "My God, have pity on me. I don't want justice. I want mercy." [52]

It is actually by repentance, confession and absolution, then, that Michael finds in his father's forgiveness release from remorse.

The final concept of justice in *They Shall Inherit The Earth* is not legalistic. Wanting at first to confess to the police so that his father will be cleared, Michael is persuaded by his wife that this is a foolish gesture. "The only justice you owe is to your father. . . . What has organized justice to do with the feeling that's in your heart?" [53] His father confirms this conviction. For although he realizes that his son's confession to the police is just by society's standard, Andrew Aikenhead prefers the hope of a growing love with Michael to the empty satisfaction of having his own innocence publicly recognized.

Symbolism is also apparent in many little ways. The names of the characters may be interpreted symbolically. In addition to Michael and Anna already noted are Andrew ("manly") Aikenhead ("Adam"), his second wife Marthe ("lordly") Choate ("plump"), her son Dave ("beloved"), and Huck Farr who in his attitude toward women clearly demonstrates that his name is meant as an obscene anagram. Literally or ironically these meanings do have significance in relation to the characters. Andrew looks back on the Eden of family love which he enjoyed twenty years before and advises his daughter Sheila: "Put your happiness with Ross ahead of everything in the world, and if you find home and your happiness are with him, that'll be your garden and it'll be the most beautiful place in the world." [54] Andrew's second wife Marthe is demanding in her relationship with him and "bit by bit made his life her life and his ways her ways." [55] Her son Dave is the only real passion of her life, and when he is drowned she is desolate.

The symbol of water, with its dual associations of death and regeneration, is developed with sensuous intensity. The reader is introduced to the pleasant lapping of the lake in the happy setting of the wine party on the sunlit beach. The same lapping water, broken by the "lonely mocking cry of a loon," is then heard as a disturbing background note to Sheila's anguished conversation with Michael over their mother's mental illness and death. After the quarrel in the boat, reminiscent of a somewhat similar scene in Dreiser's *An American Tragedy* (1925), the smooth dark water of the moonlit lake becomes a watery grave for Dave. This memory haunts Michael, who in his nightmares hears the sound of faintly lapping water, the lapping sound always getting a little louder, like the sound of small waves striking the boat in a lake in which the water was getting rougher, and then there was just the darkness of night and the vast immeasurable expanse of water. Then there was nothing to see but night, nothing but night upon the water, nothing to look at but the loneliness of night on the wide water, nothing but night, then nothing but dark water.[56]

This picture becomes inextricably associated with death. Waiting anxiously in the hospital for Anna, he "closed his eyes. He thought he could see a stretch of water in the night. He thought he could hear the lapping of water. He was sure now that she would not live." [57]

The idea of death quite naturally looms large in a novel which examines the multiple effects of a youth's drowning during a period of society in which old values and concepts are also dying. In a universe which seems stupid and meaningless, in which all the lovely things appear accidental, Michael cynically feels that death is the only absolute. Yet his association with Anna, for whom "there was something everlasting in each moment," persuades him to believe that there may be "something high and even deathless in their love for each other." [58] His thoughts in the hospital, indeed, reflect how far his concept of death as the final answer has changed:

All the ways of dying were in him then while he waited; the calm old man waiting in the winter, waiting patiently and smiling, the heroic bright willing deaths of martyrs that were not deaths, the beautiful deaths, the celebrated deaths, the gasping, choking, futile deaths of soldiers in the mud. His own mother's death was like a creeping blindness; and there were the nice, quiet deaths that made them all say gravely, "He died a beautiful death in the consolation of his religion." All such ways of dying, no doubt, had a high, proud place in the hierarchy of death; but they were not the same as the death of someone young dying in the early summer, in the time of the roses and the green grass, for whom there could be no consolation, and who cried out, "I don't want to die, oh, God, I don't want to die," and yet died while the warm winds were blowing from the south.[59]

The contemplation of death, which preoccupies Andrew as well as Michael, has also a regenerative effect. For as they individually come to accept the blame for Dave's death, their pride dies within them and with broken and contrite hearts they find together a new joy in life.

Callaghan's probing of the conditions of the Depression period is penetrating. He catches the note of fear in the minds of "workers and capitalists and priests and politicians" as they realize the coming changes. He exposes the inhumanity of the Marxist solution to individual misery. He rejects the scientific point of view as myopic and scientists as too specialized "to consider the relation of one thing to another." [60] He portrays satirically the modern businessman in the partners Andrew Aikenhead and Jay Hillquist who look back nostalgically to those "times many years ago when they were happy in a more innocent way, when they were both poor and their children were growing, when they were both in love with their wives." [61] Andrew recognizes the deceit in the advertising world, as evidenced in the scheming to get the Roebuck cheese account, and feels the gaiety of their lives to be hollow. But Jay refuses to let his business sense be affected by the dictates of his heart: "he could not imagine a society among men where there was not a ruthless struggle for profit, where man did not stand alone, and where a man did not have a sacred right to demand that he be left alone to conduct his own business in his own way." [62] His break with Andrew after the tragedy is a simple business transaction, an ironical repetition of the polite rejection by former associates at the old Richmond Club.

Appropriately for his theme Callaghan also examines the attitude of nominal Christians. Encouraged by the sympathy of the Reverend Dr. Tucker, Andrew goes alone to his church. Sitting quietly at the back,

he began to think it was wonderful the way they were all held fast together in one splendid, abiding communion while they worshipped God. He began to feel that he could truly lose himself among them, and, in losing himself, possess forever his own soul. The sound of the music and the sound of the ardent voices became like a caress. He, himself, longed to make a little prayer. Without any glibness, he whispered to himself, "I used to take pride in being different from other people. I used to like to think I was going my own way and that I was clever and that it was up to me to have my own way with the rest of the world. In my own way I was an enemy of the community because I was only interested in my own welfare. I know now how terrible it is to keep doing things that make people draw away from each other. I'm terribly sorry for anything I ever did that separated one man from another. I've had to feel a lot to see it that way, but now I know how dreadful it is to be put apart from people. It's not good to stand apart in your thinking and hoping. My God, I want to think and feel as all these people here think and feel. If I do that, then I know I'm closer to you, God." [63]

The terrible irony of Andrew's humble, if sentimental prayer is revealed when at the communion rail itself he is shunned by these fashionable Pharisees. Even the understanding compassion of Dr. Tucker has a comically ironic touch. For it springs from his own sense of humiliation over a recent altercation with a shoemaker.

The characters of *They Shall Inherit The Earth* are drawn together by a common bond of loneliness, sense of guilt and desire for security. Callaghan's portrayal is warm and understanding. Even the longings of Marthe and her son Dave are sympathetically delineated. In contrast with the restless souls of the book two characters stand out. Although they are also touched by the uncertainties of their era, Ross Hillquist and Anna Prychoda are major instruments in helping their fellow humans find meaning in life.

Recognizing the emptiness of his father's sense of values, Ross has worked out his own attitude to life. He radiates friendliness and gives the impression of possessing "his own soul in a remarkable and magnificently simple way." [64] His love for Sheila is manifested in such spontaneous gestures as picking water lilies for her. His hospitality and generosity to Mike and Anna are genuine.

Anna is even more the epitome of a warm friendliness, a "disinterested goodness," that is reflected in her eyes, her smile, the glow of her face and her eager personality. As Michael tells her, "It doesn't matter how much anybody hurts you; as soon as you feel other people are hurt you want to give all of yourself to help them." [65] Her warmth and radiance bring Michael to a resolution of his dilemma. They also free his sister from her secret fears of familial insanity so that she can give full expression to her love for her husband Ross. Anna's love obviously pours out generously from an overflowing heart. Yet the reader may be jarred by the evidence of its liberality in Anna's admission of two previous lovers before Michael. This gratuitous information not only tarnishes the angelic image of the heroine but also suggests a certain inconsistency in Anna's character: in her earlier queries about Huck Farr she is shy and virginal, and her date with him is reluctantly and despairingly made. This portrayal, however, is consistent with Callaghan's realistic approach. As he has remarked, "I don't know any pure innocents. . . . a man's nature is a very tangled web, shot through with gleams of heavenly light, no doubt, and the darkness of what we call evil forces." [66]

In both structural technique and analysis of human psychology *They Shall Inherit The Earth* is an artistic advance upon earlier novels. Its characters not only assume moral responsibility for their actions but even achieve that understanding of life for which they seek. Their thoughts and emotions are often revealed through the reflections of each other rather than by dialogue or author's description. Their own introspection is more penetrating and plausible, even though this introspection, like the dialogue, occasionally gives the impression of being ventriloquistic instead of authentic. At times the characterization is obviously manipulated: Mike's violent antagonisms build up and thaw out too quickly to appear natural. Yet the characters do retain the reader's interest and sympathy. The former straight-line chronological narrative is varied by the technique of flash-back, as exemplified in the presentation of the original development of the conflict between Michael and Andrew and the details of the first Mrs. Aikenhead's illness. The symbolism is more elaborate and more organically sustained. Even the setting has become more generalized: although the city is still obviously Toronto, although Lakewood resembles Collingwood, and Barrie is mentioned by name, the impression of a characteristically North American region is maintained. Anna, actually a native of Detroit, is "born in this country" and the cities of Boston and New York are depicted as relatively close. The result of these artistic advances is to produce a complex representation of human experience which, in spite of a certain prolixity and artificiality, has a universal rather than a local application.

CHAPTER 5

The End of an Era

EVEN while writing the novels of the early thirties Callaghan had continued to turn out short stories. These were published in such leading American magazines as *Scribner's, Harper's Bazaar, The Atlantic Monthly, Redbook, Esquire* and in particular *The New Yorker*. After his return from Paris he spent a good deal of time in New York. There he associated with editors Max Perkins of Scribner's, Bennett Cerf of Random House (who was to publish *Now That April's Here* and *More Joy In Heaven*), Harold Ross and Mrs. E. B. White of *The New Yorker*, and with writers like Thomas Wolfe, James T. Farrell, William Saroyan, Sherwood Anderson, Sinclair Lewis and William Carlos Williams. In 1936 Callaghan, along with his wife and four-year-old son Michael, lived for six months in New York. During this period he became interested in the world of drama, and was on familiar terms with a number of producers, actors and actresses.

The influence of his experiences in Paris and New York, the evidence of his shift in interest from themes of social concern to those which involved personal issues—moral, religious and political—and his artistic development over a period of a decade of writing are apparent in his second collection of short stories, *Now That April's Here* (1936) and in his last novel of the thirties, *More Joy In Heaven* (1937).

I *Now That April's Here* (1936)

Callaghan's second collection presents thirty-five selected stories written between 1929 and 1935. All of these had already been published in North American magazines except the title piece. It appeared in *This Quarter* (October-December, 1929) as the result of a bet which Edward Titus made with Callaghan and Robert McAlmon in Paris encouraging both to write a story expressing each's contrasting views about two young men familiar in the Montparnasse of 1929.[1] McAlmon never did write his story.

"Now That April's Here" comes fourth in the arrangement of the book. Its two chief characters, Charles Milford with his "large round head that ought to have belonged to a Presbyterian minister," and his younger companion Johnny Hill with his "rather chinless faun's head" arrive in Paris in the late autumn. They have left their native Middle West city convinced that the American continent has "nothing to offer them." They spend their afternoons wandering around the streets, admiring in art gallery windows such *objets d'art* as "the prints of the delicate clever unsubstantial line work of Foujita." In the evenings they sit together at the cafés, snickering at the conversation of other customers. Aspiring writers, they look forward to the stimulating spring days of April.

The story traces in dramatic interludes this autumn introduction, a winter in Nice and their eager return to Paris at the beginning of April. Ironically that month frustrates their expectations. For it brings cold and disagreeable weather, a temporary separation of the two friends as Johnny visits in England, and an irrevocable rift in their intimate relationships when Constance Foy, "a simple-minded fat-faced girl with a boy's body and short hair dyed red" becomes part of this unconventional love triangle. During the bright clear days while "Paris was gay and lively" as though in mockery of their romantic hopes, the boys are "sad and hurt and sorry." On the evening of the rainy day when Johnny leaves to return home to the United States with Constance, Charles sits forlornly at a café with his overcoat wrapped around him and wearing his large black American hat for the first time in Paris.

Throughout his depiction of these youths Callaghan carefully builds up details which authenticate the atmosphere of intimacy that surrounds his main figures as they move about the left bank circle: "People sitting at the café in the evening when the lights were on, saw them crossing the road together under the street lamp, their bodies leaning forward at the same angle and walking on tiptoe." Charles' nervous habit of "scratching his cheek with the nail of his right forefinger till the flesh was torn and raw," his way of raising his eyebrows, Johnny's manner of snickering with his finger over his mouth, and even their bedroom conversations all develop a concrete picture of their strange world. Callaghan's handling of this detail is full of clever suggestion and insinuation. Even the title has an appropriately ironic twist in terms of Browning's original application in "Home Thoughts from Abroad," as Johnny's April visit to England brings not spring joy but the autumnal decay of disintegrating family relationships, and the two boys never do "recapture / The first fine careless rapture." Yet the story has an overall mocking brittleness of tone, which is not evident in the deft treatment of a somewhat similar theme in *No Man's Meat,* and which is different from Callaghan's customary compassionate or even detached interpretation of human aberrations.

Seven of the stories in *Now That April's Here* are included in J. Edward O'Brien's *The Best Short Stories* annual editions of 1930 through 1936. Set against selections of other writers, these tales provide a criterion of Callaghan's comparative skill in the genre as well as an indication of changes in his own technique. They also treat a variety of themes which are representative of his 1936 collection: young lovers' quarrels and problems; relations between parents and children; religious and miscellaneous subjects.

"The Faithful Wife," which appeared in the December 28, 1929 issue, was the first of thirty-nine of Callaghan's stories to be published in *The New Yorker.* It is included not only in the 1930 edition of *The Best Short Stories* but also in O'Brien's *50 Best American Short Stories 1915-1939* (1939), as well as in Martha Foley's *Fifty Best American Short Stories 1915-1965* (1965). This piece catches a mood of poignant frustration. A young woman Lola, whose husband is a war invalid, invites a youthful lunch counter attendant George to her apartment on the last night before he leaves to enter college. The early winter setting is suggestively portrayed: the shoddy restaurant near the railway station, warming-up base for "brightly dressed and highly powdered" girls who are sharply contrasted with "gentle, and aloofly pleasant" Lola, and the older counter men with their knowing ways who urge on the naïve George, are realistically depicted. George's unexpected invitation to Lola's apartment and his nervous expectation are skilfully exploited as he finds Lola dressed in a tight fitting sweater and "almost savagely" responsive to his initial over-

179733

tures. Yet for her these embraces are terminal. She has correctly assessed George's temperament—that he will "not spoil it for her." The story is typical of Callaghan in its moving insight into spiritual kinship, its sharpness of detail, and the final shift of frustration from the faithful wife Lola to the reluctantly noble young man.

"The Young Priest," originally published in *The New Yorker* of September 27, 1930 and included in the 1931 edition of *The Best Short Stories,* was later modified and expanded into a chapter in *A Broken Journey.* As noted already,[2] this episode is a sensitive treatment of a young and inexperienced priest's introduction to the ugly actualities of life.

"The Red Hat," first published in the October 31, 1931 issue of *The New Yorker* and included in the 1932 edition of *The Best Short Stories,* expresses a frustrated yearning typical of the Depression era and appropriate to the autumn background against which it is set. A young wife Frances yields to the impulse to spend a great part of her weekly salary on a little red hat. Since her actor husband Eric, out of work for four months, "had been so moody and discontented recently she now thought with pleasure of pleasing him by wearing something that would give her a new elegance, of making him feel cheerful and proud of her and glad, after all, that they were married." Her eager modelling of the hat, however, precipitates a violent quarrel with Eric over the sensitive subject of money. Anxious to conciliate him, she sells the hat to the landlady for a third of its original price.

The structure moves neatly in a circle with Frances' emotions being described in both the opening and the conclusion in similar language. Just as she had let her fancies wander in front of the silver-faced and red-lipped mannequin in the shop window, so she lets her hopes rise that she can buy the hat back from Mrs. Foley and feels "an eagerness and a faint elation; it was a plain little red hat, the kind of hat she had wanted for months, elegant and expensive, a plain felt hat, but so very distinctive." Frances' desire, hesitation and finely shaded rationalization are concretely conveyed. The scene in the shop, where the "deep-bosomed saleswoman, splendidly corseted, and wearing black silk" ingratiatingly smiles approval, and Frances' vision of her own face in the mirror resembling the mannequin's face, is neatly balanced by the home scene with Eric slumped disconsolately in his chair and savagely deflating Frances' dream of his admiring approbation.

"A Sick Call," which appeared in the *Atlantic Monthly* of September, 1932 and was included in the 1933 edition of *The Best Short Stories,* probes a Roman Catholic priest's dilemma of conscience. Called to the bedside of a sick and frightened woman who has left the Church, old Father Macdowell meets the sullen opposition of her husband, John Williams. Behind the screen of his deafness, shortness of breath and tired legs, the priest succeeds in entering the bedroom which symbolically reminds him of a little girl's room with its light wall-paper with tiny birds in flight. John's protest against the priest's attempt to disrupt their spiritual kinship is futile in the face of Father Macdowell's patient persistence and even guile. Requesting a glass of water, he quickly hears Mrs. Williams' confession and gives absolution during the brief period in which her husband is out of the room getting the drink.

Throughout the story Father Macdowell is the focal figure. The significant details of his physical appearance and tolerant disposition are briefly sketched in the opening paragraph: his "wheezy breath," large build, "white-headed except for a shiny baby-pink bald spot on the top of his head," his florid face with its "fine red interlacing vein lines" and his tenderness with those who come to confess. All of these details are relevant to the bedroom scene and play a part in his battle of wits with John. Appropriately the conclusion returns to the priest as he goes home from the brief call pondering uneasily "whether he had played fair with the young man," whether he has come between the two, alternating ironically between "rejoicing amiably to think he had so successfully ministered to one who had strayed from the faith," and admiring sadly the staunch—if "pagan"—beauty of John's love for his wife.

"Mr. and Mrs. Fairbanks," first published in *Harper's Bazaar* (September, 1933) and included in the 1934 edition of *The Best Short Stories,* is a miniature drama of misunderstanding between two young married people.Walking arm in arm together in the park, they share their mixed emotions over the discovery that Helen Fairbanks is expecting a baby. Bill's pride and pleasure in his wife's condition gradually overcome her uncertainty and fear until they are both glowing with contentment. At this crucial moment they pass a bench where a tired, shabby old man is sitting looking like a beggar. In an impulsive gesture of generosity Helen offers him a quarter which he declines with simple dignity. This silent rebuke arouses in her a mood of humiliation and injured pride that Bill's logically comforting remarks only accentuate. The happy contentment of a few moments before evaporates, the afternoon sunlight becomes "hot and withering, drying up the little bit of freshness there was in the park," and fear of future poverty and old age pervades her thoughts. As the couple turn homeward, keeping "a step away from each other, so their elbows would not touch," they hurry past the bench where the old man is seated. Glancing back Helen sees him "looking after them, and suddenly he smiled at her, smiling gently as if he had noticed in the first place that they had been happy and now were like two lovers who had quarrelled." This understanding rapport restores the mutual glow shared by husband and wife.

In his portrayal of the Fairbanks Callaghan catches and registers how fragile human relationships may be. Although the background of the Depression sharpens their fears and anxieties in contemplation of the responsibilities of parenthood, the emotions represented have a universal application. Even man's response to the weather is conditioned by his feeling of the moment.

"Father and Son," published in *Harper's Bazaar*, June, 1934 and included in the 1935 edition of *The Best Short Stories*, explores the feelings of a father who after a four year interval visits a young son and his mother. Greg Henderson, moderately successful New York lawyer, is drawn by an inexplicable compulsion to the old stone farmhouse in Pennsylvania where his former wife Mona lives with her husband Frank Molsen. From the moment of his arrival Greg feels uneasily aware of how unimportant he has become in the life of Mona and his own son Mike, who is ignorant of his real parent's identity. Despite the natural antagonism between himself and Frank, Greg is able to establish a companionable relationship with Mike. Although he contemplates taking his son away with him, Greg realizes how wrong such an action would be, and takes a kind of resigned pride in the fact that Mike is a "fine boy."

This is a story of strong contrasts both in natural setting and in human characteristics. The dark hill and the shadow cast by the huge old barn stand out sharply in the moonlight and the flood of light from the window; the silence of the mist-laden valley is a sudden change for Greg who is accustomed to city noises. Tall and dark in expensive clothes, Greg is in physical contrast with Frank, short and fair in his leather jacket. Temperamentally, the distinction between the two is even more marked. Urban Greg seems lonely, wretched and out of place in the simple farm home of Mona, with her peaceful assurance, and of Frank, with his social revolutionary enthusiasm. The latter looks on this "no-account lawyer, a little bourgeois," as though "he were an old enfeebled man who had been a slave all his life." This sense of himself creeps into Greg's own mind as he listens to the symbolical sound of "the trickling of water in the nearly dried-up creek." Yet his pleasant day with his son and Mike's warm and spontaneous farewell bring a surge of joy to Greg which fills his emptiness and somehow unites him spiritually with Mona and Frank.

"The Blue Kimono," first published in the May, 1935 issue of *Harper's Bazaar* and included in the 1936 edition of *The Best Short Stories*, conveys with restraint the powerful feelings of a young couple when their son falls ill. Waking at dawn, George finds his wife Marthe nursing their feverish boy Walter, whom she suspects of having infantile paralysis. This new calamity triggers an outburst of bitterness from George over the bad luck which had dogged them ever since coming to the city. The corrosive effect of six months' unemployment on their bright dreams and aspirations, their fine resolutions and plans, seems to him to be symbolized by his wife's tattered blue kimono:

The kimono had been of a Japanese pattern adorned with clusters of brilliant flowers sewn in silk. George had given it to her at the time of their marriage; now he stared at it, torn as it was at the arms, with pieces of old padding hanging out at the hem, with the light-coloured lining showing through in many places, and he remembered how, when the kimono was new, Marthe used to make the dark hair across her forehead into bangs, fold her arms across her breasts, with her wrists and hands concealed in the sleeve folds, and go around the room in the bright kimono, taking short, prancing steps, pretending she was a Japanese girl.

As the boy's temperature drops under the effect of an aspirin, however, both father and mother gain new hope. Mutual concern for their child deepens their own love for each other. The quiet implications of this changed mood are subtly indicated as Marthe, taking off the kimono, is suddenly sure that she can "draw the torn parts together and make it look bright and new."

In "Day by Day" the discouraging effect of unemployment is particularly evident. This compact story, originally published in *The New Yorker* of August 20, 1932, treats the theme of suspicion and jealousy nourished by economic distress. Pretty young Madge Winslow, after an innocent afternoon of window-shopping, relaxes peacefully in the park and dreams of recapturing with her husband John the eager spontaneity of their days of romance. Uncomplaining of the failure of their plans "or that her husband went from one job to another and the work was always less suited to him," she timidly asks "God to make her husband content, without any suspicion of her." Arriving home late, by her very animation and inner warmth she excites a jealous outburst from John. When he walks out of the house angry and embarrassed by his violence and lack of faith, Madge sits down to await his return:

Tears were in her eyes as she looked around the mean little kitchen. She had such a strange feeling of guilt. White-faced and still, she tried to ask herself what it was that was slowly driving them apart day by day.

Accentuated by the conditions of the Depression era, the dilemma, frustration, paradox and disillusionment involved in the adjustment of a married couple are all subtly suggested or concretely portrayed; the very beauty which attracts a young man can also make him a suspicious husband; the cruel misunderstandings of married life are in stark contrast with the carefree gaiety and trust of courtship; youthful hopes often dissolve in the harsh actualities of experience; and hope itself may sometimes seem an affront to the miserable. More pervasively than many of the pieces in Callaghan's collection, "Day by Day" reflects the mood of pessimism of the thirties which intensified the age-old problems of young lovers.

When he was requested in 1942 to select his own favorite story for Whit Burnett's collection of "over 150 self-chosen and complete masterpieces" from "America's 93 living authors" published in *This Is My Best* (1943), Callaghan submitted "Two Fishermen." This story treats a typically Callaghan theme of human justice through an interesting series of ironic contrasts. Young Michael Foster, only reporter for the small town *Examiner*, discovers the identity of the man K. Smith who has arrived to hang Michael's old acquaintance Thomas Delaney, convicted of killing his wife's molester. In an evening of fishing together Michael and Smitty come to understand each other. The next morning after the hanging in the jail Smitty magnanimously gives to Michael two fish caught that morning. Shortly afterwards outside the jail yard these same fish are seized by one of the angry crowd and thrown at the hangman.

The peaceful setting of Collingwood on Georgian Bay, with "the blue hills beyond the town . . . shining brilliantly on square patches of farm land," seems incongruous with the hangman's grim purpose. In his explanation of why he chose this story for inclusion in *This Is My Best* Callaghan comments on the warm human relationship which developed between the young reporter and the executioner, as well as

the hangman's rather wistful attachment to his despised job and his realization that it gave him an opportunity to get around the country and enjoy himself as a human being and a fisherman. And then after I had written it I saw that it had a certain social implication that I liked. The hangman, a necessary figure in society, a man definitely serving the public and the ends of justice, was entitled to a little human dignity. In fact he saw himself as a dignified human being. But of course as an instrument of justice he became a despised person, and even his young friend, who understood his wistful humanity, betrayed that humanity when the chips were down. If I had started out to write the story with that in mind it might have become very involved but I wrote it very easily and naturally and without any trouble at all.

The contrast between Smitty in his human aspect and Mr. K. Smith as a public official is striking. As a fisherman dressed in casual clothes he is a small shy man "with little gray baby curls on the back of his neck," proud father of five children and an amusing raconteur. As an executioner "dressed in a long black cut-away coat with gray striped trousers, a gates-ajar collar and a narrow red tie" he walks with military precision and carries himself "with a strange cocky dignity." These two aspects of his personality are neatly brought together in the image of the two fish which he gives to Michael. They exemplify for both Michael and Smitty the fact that man is not only an individual but is also a creature of society. The fish, symbolical evidence of friendship, also become in the closing episode instruments of human betrayal and shameful rejection.

The stories of *Now That April's Here* have a remarkably uniform quality. The themes of the remaining twenty-five will be briefly noted. Several treat a variety of dreams, misunderstandings or entanglements of lovers: "The Rejected One," a family's disapproval of a young man's gaudy belle as a suitable marriage partner; "Guilty Woman," a young woman's stolen moment of love with her older sister's sweetheart; "Let Me Promise You," the attempt to recapture a former beau by an expensive birthday present; "Ellen," an unmarried pregnant woman's hope that her lover will return; "Timothy Harshaw's Flute," a young couple's impractical dream of moving to Paris; "The Snob," a lovers' quarrel resulting from a young man's sense of shame in snubbing his poor father; "The Two Brothers," the complex influence of a prodigal upon his older brother's love affair; "The Bride," the need for mutual attention in marriage; "One Spring Night," the natural warmth and the frustration of adolescent love; "It Must Be Different," the stifling effect of parental suspicion on young love; "Younger Brother," a boy's ignorant confusion about his sister's attitude to men; "Three Lovers," an older man's loss of his loved one to a younger rival through lack of trust; "The Duel," a former beau's failure to win back his girl; "Silk Stockings," a frustrated attempt to win a girl's approval by a birthday present; "Rigmarole," the need to preserve in married love the sentimentalities of courtship; and "Possession," the recognition that a woman's genuine concern for her lover is superior to mere physical surrender.

Other stories in the collection reflect Callaghan's understanding of family life and the relationship between parents and children. The initial story, "All the Years of Her Life," which was included in *Short Stories from The New Yorker* (1940), presents a double exposure of a mother whose son is detected in petty larceny. Her public display of courageous dignity and calm strength as she dissuades his employer from prosecuting are balanced in her own home by a private expression of frightened despair and trembling weakness. The effect of family dissension on both parents and children is portrayed in "The Runaway," in which the quarrels of his father and stepmother so magnify a boy's own little failures that he runs away. "A Separation" reveals the unhappy result of a broken home and the tensions which arise between a deserted husband and his son.

The remaining pieces concern diverse aspects of human aspiration, disappointment and adjustment. In "Shining Red Apple" a fruit dealer gives vent to his resentment over not having a son by tormenting a hungry boy. "Lunch Counter" dramatizes the suspicions of a frustrated sensualist and his prudish wife who spoil an innocent friendship between a cook and a teen-age girl. In "Rocking Chair" the symbol of a young widower's love for his deceased wife is misinterpreted by an aggressive female friend as a token of favor toward her. "An Old Quarrel" contrasts the significance of petty animosities of bygone days with the richness of memories of happy times together. A priest's visit in "Absolution" arouses in an alcoholic woman "a faintly remembered dignity" of past respectability. In "Sister Bernadette" an illegitimate baby becomes the symbol of the sacrificed motherhood of a hospital nun.

Now That April's Here indicates both continuity and change in Callaghan's fictional technique. As in his earlier *A Native Argosy*, the stories, although distinctive and individual in flavor, do follow a recognizable formula. They are all self-contained anecdotes. Their opening is usually a declarative statement that sets the stage for a drama that most frequently is psychological and involves little action. A problem is posed, and, by description, dialogue and internal monologue, the story moves with easy economy through a climax to an ending which may not resolve the dilemma but invariably leaves it haunting the reader's mind. Sometimes the conclusion returns full cycle to the same emotional attitudes introduced initially, and these are then perceived in the light of a changed situation. Few violent passions are depicted, and little humor is displayed except in the quiet irony which pervades the style. A sure sense of significant detail and mood, and an unobtrusive use of symbolism contribute suggestive overtones of universality.

There are, however, obvious changes in the stories of this second collection. The chronological duration is briefer. The settings are authentically American, since many of the stories were actually written in New York about that city, and its streets are often mentioned by name. The tales reflect the conditions of the Depression era. The depiction of family life involving children is more frequent. The syntax is tighter and the overall structure more artful than in A Native Argosy. The characters, although still unpretentious and ordinary people, are generally more intelligent and more sophisticated than the bewildered persons of earlier stories with whom the average reader has difficulty identifying himself. Callaghan interprets this cross-section of humanity with sympathy yet detachment. His tales have a restraint, an unstressed reticence and a deceptive gentleness that subtly convey to the reader the quiet implications of the awkward emotional predicaments and fluctuations between happiness and despair which occur in intimate relationships. In his adroit handling of those commonplace actions that involve failure to adjust to circumstances or personalities, Callaghan in these later stories leaves the reader with a profound awareness of a universal truth: respect for individual dignity, patience and understanding love provide the best solution to the problems of life.

II *More Joy in Heaven* (1937)

Like *Such Is My Beloved* and *They Shall Inherit The Earth*, this novel takes its title from the New Testament, explores again love and justice in human society, and the action is underlined by religious symbolism. The immediate inspiration for *More Joy in Heaven*, however, was the actual case history of a celebrated Canadian convict, the final stage of whose career is summarized by Professor Hugo McPherson in his Introduction to the "New Canadian Library" edition.

On July 24, 1935, the notorious gunman and bank robber, Red Ryan, was released from Kingston Penitentiary after serving eleven and a half years of a life sentence. It had taken the combined efforts of a devoted priest, a senator, a hotel owner, some Toronto Kiwanians, and the

Prime Minister of Canada, the Right Honourable R. B. Bennett, to secure Ryan's ticket-of-leave. They were certain that he was a completely reformed man—a paragon; and his native Toronto welcomed him home with the extravagance of a father embracing a prodigal son. Financiers and sportsmen soon associated with Ryan on familiar terms; he became an automobile salesman and the official greeter at the Nealton Hotel on King Street—a night club which featured singing waiters.

Ten months later, on May 23, 1936, Ryan was shot to death by police while attempting to rob a liquor store in Sarnia.

Although this sequence was the stimulus for the novel, the back of the title page reminds the reader that "The characters and situations in this novel are entirely fictional, and do not represent or portray any actual persons or events." Callaghan himself, moreover, remarked years later that his story was not simply a dramatization of a criminal's unhappy end: "The idea was the same, except that what made me tired during that period was that everybody went around saying society is betrayed—you know, that Red Ryan betrayed society. This always bores me. I don't think society is ever betrayed." [3]

The theme emerges early in the novel: the repentance of a sinner or the return of a prodigal is an occasion for feasting, but his permanent rehabilitation is a difficult and complex process. *More Joy in Heaven* treats a social problem that the individual himself cannot solve. Kip Caley, released on Christmas day from prison through the efforts of Senator Maclean and Father Butler, returns to his home town anxious to start a new life. People feel a warm and sentimental generosity toward him, a comfortable sense of self-justification at the repentance of a notorious sinner. Their well-meaning benevolence, however, is without any purposeful beneficence. After the first flush of public interest in his home-coming, he no longer attracts patrons to the tavern where he works as a host and its owner Jenkins tries dishonestly to exploit Kip. Senator Maclean, "reckless exhibitionist" and "man of irresponsible generosity," becomes absorbed in new enthusiasms and his own personal problems. Judge Ford, who originally sentenced Kip, still regards him as incorrigible and refuses to believe that his desire to help rehabilitate former convicts is sincere. Even his closest friends, Julie Evans and Father Butler, momentarily lack the faith to trust completely his genuine change of heart. Within three months Kip dies as the result of a gunfight, as much a martyr of loyalty as the victim of his own *hamartia,* his fatal flaw of violence and his need for dramatic recognition.

The intense irony of Kip's failure is accentuated by the religious symbolism, which remains subordinate to the created drama. The parable of the lost sheep in Luke ends with the comment that "there will be more joy in heaven over one sinner who repents than over ninety-nine righteous persons who need no repentance." Then follows the story of the faithless steward with its moral, "you cannot serve God and Mammon," and the parable of the prodigal son at whose return his father rejoices, "for this my son was dead and is alive again." In the next chapter is drawn the contrast between the life, and especially the after-life, of the rich man and the beggar Lazarus. In the bosom of Abraham, Lazarus is comforted, while the rich man in Hades is tormented by thirst. His request that his living brothers be warned by Lazarus of the punishment in store for the uncharitable is denied. Abraham's reply is, "If they do not hear Moses and the prophets, neither will they be convinced if some one should rise from the dead."

In keeping with this underlying motif of regeneration the novel opens on the dawn of a Christmas day which for Kip is "the most beautiful morning in all history." Riding away from the prison, Senator Maclean reflects on his part in securing Kip's parole: "It's like handing him a new life." One of the reporters covering the return remarks to Kip, "Your birthday," and he himself feels in the reunion with his mother "the beautiful beginning of his new life." Ironically called "the light of the world" by his former prison associate and satanic tempter, Joe Foley, Kip is Christ-like in his aspiration to help his fellowmen. He is tempted, but during a lonely vigil resists temptation. Even his death is related to this Christian symbolism. Shot down in the Easter season with two thieves whom he sought to save, he reaffirms his love for those who brought him sacrificial death, and then lingers silently for three days in the hospital. Outside, the crowd who such a short time before had hailed him as a hero in the tavern—significantly decorated with palm trees—now cry for his blood:

It was necessary that he be hanged in order that their pride and self-respect might be redeemed, that they might be cleansed of their humiliation, and that the pattern of law and order be finally imposed upon him. . . . "Hasn't he said anything?". . . They were outraged that he didn't pray that they forgive him.[4]

Kip Caley, as the novel's title suggests, is the reclaimed sinner over whom heaven rejoices. He is jestingly referred to as "the repentant one" by Foley, of whom Father Butler remarks, "If he could get Kip back with him he'd feel like a shepherd who had found a lost sheep."[5] Judge Ford sternly rejects the public's acclaim of Kip's reformation by commenting, "There's more joy on earth than there is in heaven."[6]

Even more than the lost sheep discovered, though, Kip is the prodigal son, who after a wild and lawless life comes to himself in prison. The return to his own family circle is clouded by the uncertainty and fears of his mother and younger brother Denis, but society's welcome is so extravagant that Kip is initially embarrassed. He is reassured, however, by Senator Maclean's enthusiasm and by Bishop Murray's reminder, "after all, they did a little feasting and celebrating for the prodigal son."[7] Accepting the Bishop's cue, Kip explains to Julie Evans, "Maybe we're all prodigal sons, everybody on earth, see, going away places and feeling homesick and wanting to come back."[8] On New Year's Eve at the Coronet Hotel he is spontaneously applauded by the crowd as the "apotheosis" of its best resolutions: "He seemed to become the prodigal son of the whole country."[9]

Identifying himself completely with this role, Kip is astonished that Father Butler should suggest leaving the city for the quiet job of parish gardener:

"Listen, what would you have thought of the prodigal son if he had come home, and found his old man and his family had got a big feast ready and invited all the neighbors in and they were all getting ready for a swell time, and the son takes one look at them and refuses to sit down on account of them wanting to make a fuss over him? . . . A killjoy—too dumb and self-centered to see it didn't mean anything, unless he met them half way."

The troubled priest can only reply: "Maybe the prodigal son had a job going from feast to feast till the end of his days. . . . I wonder what happened to him after the feasting was over."[10]

Ironically Kip discovers his own answer to this question. In the bitterness of his disillusionment he explains to Foley the probable fate of the prodigal son:

"He sat around for months and months and it all wore off and he got fed up and bored and disgusted and . . . saw that the big feeling he had was just a shot in the arm for the folks of the town, then he cleared out, hating everybody, and back he went to the happy hunting ground." [11]

Yet this is not the ultimate destiny of Kip. His change of heart in prison was genuine.

The artistic genius of Callaghan is revealed in his meaningful interpretation of the traditional story. The real return of this prodigal is not to his family or to society at large, but to the spiritual home of his Heavenly Father. After his lonely Gethsemane in the streets all night, when he conquers the temptation to join in the bank robbery attempt, Kip knows that his inner convictions of right "don't depend on anyone else." Even after his betrayal he is drawn home to that divine love revealed in the personalities of Father Butler and especially Julie Evans. Hiding in the coal cellar after killing the policeman, Kip realizes that although his death is sure the memory of Julie is "the bright, living part of him." Towards her he painfully drags himself through back alleys, "longing for home." [12] Despite the waiting ambush he succeeds in climbing the apartment stairs to reaffirm to her, "You brought me life." [13] Even her death cannot touch the peace he has made "with Julie and the things he knew were good." [14]

There is a passing allusion to the parable of the rich man and Lazarus, but its symbolical impact is less direct than that of the two previous parables already discussed. Its introduction, indeed, is misleading, for Kip's mention of the name is in connection with that Lazarus, brother of Mary and Martha, who like Kip "rose from the dead." [15] The story of beggar Lazarus, however, is recalled shortly after this remark when Kip sends a real beggar sprawling in the road, as well as in the relationship with the rich Senator Maclean, who tosses crumbs to Kip and whose final appearance in the hell of his alcoholic illness contrasts sharply with Kip's peaceful death.

Throughout the novel Kip is pictured as a huge, powerful and primitive animal. In court at the time of his sentence he is described as "a big black bull." He is confined behind bars in the prison where the lashes stripe his body like that of a beast. Shown his room at the Coronet Hotel, he feels "as if he had been suddenly pushed into a cage." In this room the "sound of his feet padding on the carpet as he walked up and down made him feel he was in a cage" [16] and that the hotel was a "menagerie." In his final return to Julie he "creeps along in the shadow" like a skulking animal whose "breathing was labored and desperate like a tired dog's." [17]

The imagery of trains is suggestively employed. Kip is fascinated by the sounds and sights associated with them. The hooting of an engine and "the rattle and swing of the cars" recall his days of violence:

. . . riding the rods bound west, his face cut to pieces with the cinders, the big meals in the club cars with the boys on that big spending trip to New York; his hands handcuffed to the detective, that trip down to the penitentiary; the everlasting night that first year lying awake in the cell and listening for the sound of the freight train, the wheels gathering speed, the swinging through the dark. [18]

Railway metaphors, which are also used by Foley, Jenkins and Julie, spring naturally to Kip's mind in referring to his career as having jumped "the tracks somewhere," to his position at the Coronet Hotel as "spanning both sides of the tracks" and to his disillusionment as "the end of the line." Standing in a mood of humiliation and despair on a railway bridge as a train approaches, he leans over eagerly toward a kind of private Inferno: "the black smoke rose up and engulfed him in the shriek of the whistle, in a belch of fire right underneath him." [19] Later his mother's death calls up in his mind an image which makes all the events of his return seem like a journey on a train:

The time when he got on the train in the prison, the hotel, a station where he changed and got on another train, still going, everything flicking past him, bright, exciting, the stop-off with the Judge. "Change here, change here, all aboard. I lost my ticket, mister. Where does this train go, mister? I'm on the wrong train, let me off, let me off, where's the next stop? I want a transfer. Why don't you stop it, blow the whistle, pull that bell." It had brought him here to his mother's death, the end of the line. He had to step out. They were there waiting for him.[20]

The blackness of train smoke, of rivers at night, of shadows and of the coal cellar where Kip hides are contrasted with the whiteness of snow, of sunlit playgrounds with innocent children, of lighted rooms and with the penetratingly bright beams of electric lights. In these contrasts is suggested the struggle between good and evil. This underlying imagery of opposing colors is intensely realized in two particular scenes. Kip's visit to the ice carnival as guest of Senator Maclean begins with the spotlights glistening on a champion skater's "oiled black hair and on his white silk blouse." In this alternation of brilliant light and shadows, Kip's companions take on an unreal aspect: "These faces were bright masks. The Senator's mask was pink and white." His daughter Ellen "had on a sharp, pretty little frozen-faced mask." Kip himself seemed like "a great crag of basalt." If in this episode the contrast of colors brings out the falseness of the *beau monde,* in another context the same basic imagery illuminates Kip's groping conscience. When a light pierces the dark coal cellar, it penetrates his conscience like a divine ray, arousing an eagerness to reassure Julie of his continuing loyalty to those ideals which have united them.

Many individually evocative images add richness to the narrative. Triangular relationships, in which Kip is the constant factor, suggest the underlying tension. The repetition of the number three is typical of Callaghan's technique. In addition to those incidents already noted which echo the New Testament, there are similar examples of behavior or remarks which recall the life of Jesus. Kip welcomes generously the admiring youngsters on his return home. He wipes Julie's feet by a moonlit pond in a narrow ravine. In this romantically pastoral setting she is reminded of phrases from Francis Thompson's "An Arab Love-Song" which in their suggestive overtones link the nomadic career of Kip with that of Ruth and Christ:

> Leave thy father, leave thy mother
> And thy brother;
>
> . . . .
>
> And thou—what needest with thy tribe's black tents
> Who hast the red pavilion of my heart?

In contrast with Kip's peaceful freedom in this home of Julie's heart is his anguished cry in flight, "Jesus Christ. . . . There's no place, no place in the world" to lay one's head. Kip's progress as a pilgrim is suggested in his climb up the stairs of Julie's apartment, stairs which contrast with those leading up "to Foley's place above the delicatessen store," or "the badly lighted flight" up to the Three Star Club, or "the stairs to the Ping Pong pool parlor." Out of the darkness of the night and of the enclosing forces of the world, Kip propels himself up that illuminated staircase. At the top wait Julie and Father Butler whose human love has prefigured the divine love of the Heavenly Father to whom Kip is returning.

Over all this symbolism there is a constant play of irony and satire. The contrast between Kip's triumphant home-coming and his ignominious death is sharp: "The bishop he had had lunch with ordered that he be buried in unconsecrated ground." The crowd's change from spontaneous welcome to vindictive desire for revenge, the injustice of Julie's death at the hands of the police, the frantic attempts by transfusions to save Kip's life so that he will not cheat the hangman, and the self-justification of society outraged at the betrayal of its generous instincts, all emphasize the tragedy of Kip's unwitting failure.

The novel's melodramatic climax is made plausible and even inevitable by Callaghan's skilful characterization. Kip is given dimension by the symbols and images. Each setting or incident in which he is depicted functions organically to reveal his terrible dilemma. Even as a youth he had experienced a "big special feeling" which made him think he was different and could make his own rules. A leader among other youngsters, at nine he had stolen a bicycle. His nature craved excitement:

He was going around like a fire horse waiting for the sound of the bell. Bank robbing came easy and it gave him everything he wanted, direct action, money, excitement, women, a rush across the country with his fame following, and the newspapers full of his pictures and stories celebrating his audacity and courage.[21]

The order and solitude of prison and the help of Father Butler had encouraged Kip to examine his life, to modify his selfish egotism and to join himself with the life of his comrades and guards.

This gesture had brought an inner peace and freedom which were reflected in his co-operative behavior and became the grounds for his parole.

Released from prison, he wants only the opportunity to lead an ordinary life. The demands of society, however, thwart his innocent desire. The press makes headlines of his reformed spirit and sparks the dream that Kip can help other convicts; Senator Maclean arranges a job that keeps Kip in the limelight and encourages in him the quixotic mission of serving on the Parole Board; his home town folk idealize him as a symbol of their faith in man's innate goodness. These very circumstances which make him a plaster saint also lead to his destruction. For they nourish that "big special feeling," that *hubris* which Kip had overcome in prison. The publicity and even the loftiness of his ambition make the puritanical Judge Ford oppose Kip's appointment to the Parole Board. The Judge's uncharitable lack of faith, although based on a shrewd insight into Kip's character, triggers in him an outburst of his old reckless violence. Just as his passion in this humiliating experience with Judge Ford is matched by that displayed in the wrestling bout with Steinbeck, so the initial blow to Kip's hopes dealt by Judge Ford is climaxed in the disillusionment brought about by Jenkins' offer of a rigged contract.

The reader follows the subsequent anguished struggle for perspective and stability in a world of crumbling dreams and ideals with fascination, compassion and eventually horror. Callaghan presents sensitively and dramatically in Kip's honest quest for values the complexity of man's nature, his aspiration and limitation, his creativity and destructiveness. The portrayal of the bewildering influences which play upon Kip's eagerly receptive but naïve mind makes understandable his confusion:

. . . the big parties, the studious little groups, then sitting in Mayor Wills' office, going everywhere with friendly laughter, into fine discussions about prisons that lasted till dawn. They kept coming from far away, a stream of eager faces flowing past him in the hotel, too many to remember, doctors, lawyers, clergymen, and the publisher who came and got him to sign a contract to write a book. Each night widened it out further; hockey games with the Macleans, the fight crowds, that fine night they introduced him from the ring and he shook hands with the two lightweights; that night he got sore at the man from the insurance company and the automobile salesmen who offered him jobs.[22]

Kip's career is a penetrating, and, indeed, Callaghan's most ferocious commentary on human justice. Kip's early lawlessness is rightfully punished by a prison term. His genuine reform is doubted by all those who are in a position to make it enduring. The reporters, hungry for sensational headlines, distrust his intentions. The Bishop "as a Christian . . . had to believe it possible in a man to change the pattern of his life, but he knew it hardly ever happened and he held aloof." To Judge Ford "justice is like a pattern—the pattern of the common good. It's up to me to see that the pattern isn't broken—just for the sake of fitting you into it. That's exactly why I thought you ought to stay in prison and finish your sentence." [23] To Kip, with his dream of helping discouraged ex-convicts in their rehabilitation, this lack of faith is akin to the cynicism of the habitual criminal Joe Foley. In society's pattern of justice there seems to be a place for the shady mining deals of Senator Maclean and the crooked wrestling contracts of Jenkins. The enforcers of this justice, too, are more interested in trapping criminals than in preventing crime. It is this irresponsible force, which can shoot down Kerrmann and Foley in cold blood, that Kip rejects in his lethal gesture of defiance. His act almost appears justified when the police themselves, with apparent immunity, murder the innocent Julie because she comes between them and their target Kip. Their legal murder passes unnoticed, while their chief ironically remarks of Kip, "it's important to the fundamentally decent human instincts in everybody that this man should be legally hanged." [24] Significantly, this vindictive expression of justice is far removed from that spiritual concept shared by Kip and Father Butler in which "a man could violate the law in such a way his goodness would not be broken, but would be strengthened; charity came before law and order." [25]

Even though Senator Maclean, Judge Ford and Bishop Murray are almost caricatures, the other characters are memorable. The story has a haunting impact. In the final chapters of the novel the style, which is throughout concrete, varied and rich in vivid description, becomes taut and suspenseful. Kip's "betrayal" by his closest friends, his failure to warn Foley and Kerrmann in time about the police trap, his escape from the police, their pursuit and his return to Julie are thrillingly depicted. The terrible anomaly of his position and the irony of the brutality shown by the forces of justice accentuate the pathos of the lovers' moving reunion and of their tragic deaths. Although painful, the dénouement of *More Joy in Heaven* is powerful and convincing.

CHAPTER 6

The Dark Period

FOR NEARLY ten years after the publication of *More Joy in Heaven* Callaghan's creative energy flagged. The outlook for civilization was grim. Hitler's persecution of the Jews, Mussolini's brutal conquest of Ethiopia in 1935, Hitler's march into the Rhineland in 1936 and his *Anschluss* with Austria in 1938, the bloody Civil War in Spain from 1936 to 1939, the growing strength of Stalin's Communism and the outbreak of World War II all combined to have a depressing effect on Callaghan. He has described this time as "the dark period of my life" and as "a period of spiritual dryness." [1]

I *Dramatic Interlude*

After 1937, for the first time in his career as a recognized author, Callaghan had difficulty writing his stories. He turned his talent to articles and reviews which reflect his thoughts and feelings about contemporary events during those years. He rejected Aldous Huxley's concept of a United Nations of pacifists, as expressed in *Ends and Means* (1938), on the grounds that it was impracticable "as long as men are not angels." [2] The Russian-German non-aggression pact, which must have seemed like "an obscene betrayal" to those intellectuals and idealists of the world who looked to Russia as the great bulwark against Fascism and Nazism, illustrated that "No set of ideas can be at all effective unless there is personal integrity and some sense of human dignity among the leaders." [3] Reviewing *The Web and the Rock* (1939), Callaghan praised Wolfe's gusto, passion and wide-eyed eagerness for life and regretted his friend's untimely death in 1938. [4] Brooding on the destructiveness of war, in December of 1939 he wrote: "If civilization must be saved," it is not enough to hide away the art treasures; the nations should also "guard with loving care their young men of creative genius," for those who make life beautiful are the true "key men" in any civilization.[5]

During this period of literary obscurity, however, not all Callaghan's ability was channeled into such noncreative writing. In 1939 he was encouraged by producer Lawrence Langner of the New York Theatre Guild to convert the novel *They Shall Inherit The Earth* into a play. Already familiar with contemporary drama, Callaghan took up this challenge eagerly. The adaptation, initially entitled "Turn Again Home" and later renamed "Going Home," was sold in January of 1940 to the New York Theatre Guild. Although it was rehearsed for production and Callaghan received advance royalties on it, the play ran into casting and financial difficulties which prevented its production by the Theatre Guild. It was not until the spring season of 1950, indeed, that this unpublished play was performed by the New Play Society under the direction of production manager J. Mavor Moore at the Museum Theatre Stage, Toronto.

"Going Home" is divided into three acts with three different Canadian settings. The first act and the first scene of the second act take place on the dock of Andrew Aikenhead's country home at an Ontario lake. The remainder of Act II is set in the lounge of the third-rate hotel in Toronto where Mike lives. Act III unfolds in the privacy of Anna's room in the same hotel. The richness of setting of *They Shall Inherit The Earth* is thus diminished by the exigencies of drama.

The range and depth of human passions explored are similarly restricted. "Going Home" concentrates mainly on the theme of a son's buried hatred for, and chance of revenge upon, his father, and the eventual reconciliation of the two. In the modifications required for the stage the motivations of the chief characters are sometimes vaguely presented. The character of Marthe Choate is even completely altered: no longer sympathetically portrayed as in the novel, she becomes a calculating schemer. A similar type of change which the drama suggested from the novel's intention is exemplified in an interesting variant version with which Callaghan toyed, in which Andrew Aikenhead, rather than his son Michael, is responsible for Dave's death by drowning.

In 1939 Callaghan wrote a second play, originally called "Just Ask for George" and later entitled "To Tell the Truth." This drama was also billed to be produced in New York but waited for some ten years before its presentation in the spring season of 1949 by the New Play Society, again under the direction of J. Mavor Moore. It was more popular than "Going Home," and after its successful première moved to the full-time professional Royal Alexandra Theatre of Toronto.

"To Tell the Truth," set somewhere in the northeastern states, dramatizes the story of a young Canadian, George, who crosses the United States border in search of that excitement and adventure which he misses at home. This open-faced extrovert finds a job as a counterman in a shoddy beanery. In his search for friendship in a world of cynicism and criticism he invents tales which make him enemies as well as friends. His experience is really an examination of "What is Truth?" in North American civilization. In a sub-plot, which underlines the theme of the main plot, George becomes involved with a gambler's mistress seeking escape from her situation.

"To Tell the Truth" is more a play of discussion than of action. Its study of character is imaginative and characteristically ironic. The hero, who is really a poet by temperament, creates a world of fantasy which is juxtaposed with unpleasant actuality. Like Timothy Harshaw in *Now That April's Here* and Warden Tyndall of *The Varsity Story*, George plays a flute. Callaghan once remarked: "The flute seems to me a symbol. The guy who plays a flute strikes a blow against the world. It has something to do with the lightness and airiness of the human spirit." [6] The pied piper picaro of this drama, by handing out free coffee to needy customers, ironically defeats the exploitation of cheap labor by his cynical employer Schultz. The appropriately tough dialogue is full of symbolism and is frequently lyrical in its flow. Although written before the presentation of *The Time of Your Life* (1939), Callaghan's play undoubtedly suffered by the inevitable comparison it invited with that of William Saroyan because of the similarities in theme, characters and underlying philosophy.

During the early years of the war Callaghan participated in a variety of efforts. In 1940 he became a regular contributor to Toronto's *New World Magazine* to which he submitted monthly commentaries until it was absorbed in 1948 into *National Home Monthly*. In 1942 he went to sea for the summer in a Royal Canadian Navy corvette to do a script for the National Film Board. In 1943 he was invited by the Canadian Broadcasting Corporation to be chairman of a new radio program which was originally called "Things to Come" and was later known as "Citizen's Forum." Its controversial discussions are credited with stimulating the establishment of a library in one town, a juvenile court in another, and with focusing attention on such thorny questions as fair employment practices. Callaghan travelled across Canada with this program for four years and came to know his own country in a new way. In 1947 he joined the panel of a CBC radio quiz show, "Beat the Champs," and began to take part in television programs. In this year, too, he resumed his primary career as a writer of fiction and once more started producing short stories. It was the success of one of these that led to the publication of his first novel since the beginning of the war.

II *Luke Baldwin's Vow* (1948)

"Luke Baldwin's Vow" appeared as a short story in *The Saturday Evening Post* in 1947. Originally submitted under the same title which it carries in *Morley Callaghan's Stories* (1959) of "The Little Business Man," the tale caught the fancy of the publisher who suggested that it be revised and expanded into a short novel. This suggestion resulted in the production of *Luke Baldwin's Vow*, which is divided into fifteen chapters, suitably titled for juvenile readers, and contains illustrations by Stanley Turner.

The novel works out through Luke's experiences the theme of a boy's reconciliation of the wonderful world of fancy with the practical world of common sense. When widower Dr. Baldwin dies of a heart attack, his son moves from the city to the home of Dr. Baldwin's brother just outside Collingwood on Georgian Bay. Childless Uncle Henry and Aunt Helen are kind and loving, but for this thirteen-year-old boy the change from city to small town is sharpened by the contrast between memories of his father's imaginative outlook on life and the utilitarian viewpoint of his uncle.

The story moves rapidly from its beginning in May to its conclusion in August. Through Luke's own thoughts and feelings his maturation is portrayed in the series of emotional crises and external problems which he encounters and resolves. His father's sudden death, Luke's loneliness and need for understanding companionship, his desire for his own secret world peopled by rustlers, pirates and even spirits, his discovery that society disapproves of carefree happiness, the trials which accompany his acceptance by his own age group, his painful awareness that "the things that made his life entertaining and often magical were the useless things according to Uncle Henry," [7] and his final discovery of how to protect what is really valuable are all presented with economy and suspense.

The characters are few. After the initial chapter the action revolves mainly around Luke, burly Uncle Henry, plump Aunt Helen, the old one-eyed collie Dan, and the wise neighbour Alex Kemp. Two other circles also play a part in Luke's growth: the mill hands of Uncle Henry's sawmill—represented primarily by dull, glum Sam Carter and happy but irresponsible Willie Stanowski with his merry eight children; and the gang of schoolboys with whom Luke plays—chiefly represented by bossy Elmer Highbottom and to a less extent by muscular Eddie Shore. The dialogue of all these characters not only appropriately reflects their personalities, but it also catches the authentic note of small-town talk. Luke's speech and internal monologue are particularly rich and varied, ranging through poignancy, unconscious irony and sly humor.

Luke Baldwin's Vow is a warm story full of excitement as well as wisdom for young readers. Luke's defense of his gentle pet Dan against the attack of Elmer Highbottom's wild dog Thor and the rescue of Dan from the bottom of the river—after the attempted drowning by mill hand Sam Carter—are moving and thrillingly suspensive episodes. The descriptions of the picturesque setting have the appeal of freshness as seen through Luke's eyes. The tale is framed by the hauntingly beautiful background of the Blue Mountains, symbolically employed as an example of the illusions against which Uncle Henry is ever on guard, and the enticing foreground of sparkling Georgian Bay, with its ships from faraway ports and its legendary Christian Island, where significantly a band of Indians had held out against a more powerful tribe. The middle ground is occupied by the sawmill, with its piercing whine, "thick golden carpet of sawdust" and "the fresh clean smell of newly cut wood," Uncle Henry's white and green house with the large veranda, Mr. Kemp's red brick house and gleaming white cowsheds, and on all sides the cool groves of thick woods. Town life is depicted in the bustling shipyard and grain elevators, the ball games and the agricultural fair.

For adults who, like Callaghan, have spent summer holidays with relatives in a setting similar to the Collingwood area, *Luke Baldwin's Vow* has a nostalgic charm. It recalls memories of a pastoral age apparently untouched by war or real vice. The important events are all innocent pleasures: exploring woods and rounding up cows with a faithful dog as companion, jumping from a roof into a pile of sawdust, hitching short rides on freight trains, listening to sailors' yarns of distant places, and dreaming happily on the veranda in rocking chair or hammock. In this novel, although two worlds clash, they both are peopled by kind and generous characters. Luke learns, moreover, how to reconcile the one with the other. For although Uncle Henry, like Plato, may reject fairy tales and pirate stories as lies, his acceptance of Luke's proposition to pay for "useless" Dan's feed reveals to Luke the secret that imagination and common sense are not incompatible. His final vow is to ensure that the magical world will never be destroyed:

Putting his head down on the dog's neck, he vowed to himself fervently that he would always have some money on hand, no matter what became of him, so that he would be able to protect all that was truly valuable from the practical people in the world.[8]

III *The Varsity Story* (1948)

In 1948 Callaghan published *The Varsity Story*, with illustrations by Eric Aldwinckle. Requested by the University of Toronto to write "a piece" for a fund-raising campaign, Callaghan responded generously by producing a fictionalized account of the complex college federation of that university and by donating the royalties from this publication to the fund. He describes the book as "a novel told in a personal way." It is actually more of a documentary of the University of Toronto's traditions, particularized by incidents of human interest as seen through the eyes of the central fictional figure Arthur Tyndall, appointed in the autumn of 1924 as Warden of Hart House, center of student community life for men.

Tyndall, a New Zealander whose visit to the majestic Algoma Hills had led him to expect a similar grandeur in Toronto, is initially disappointed by his impressions of its university. His curiosity and inner doubts about the function of such an institution, its complex organization and proper operation, its distinctive intellectual pattern and even the nature of Canadians in general prompt him to pose a series of Socratic questions which call forth answers that form the substance of the book.

Although he is not successful in fictionalizing the tradition, history and detail of the University of Toronto, Callaghan does succeed in presenting a shrewd assessment of the different autonomous arts colleges and in making an appealing case for a liberal education. Victoria College, founded by the Methodists, is portrayed as representative of independence of thought, tolerance and defense of the "semi-underprivileged." University College, originally Anglican and later non-denominational, devoting itself to "the quest for truth for truth's sake alone," Trinity College, "fed by the stream of pure religion" of the Anglican Church, and St. Michael's College, bastion of Aristotle, St. Augustine and St. Thomas, with its internationally known Medieval Institute, are all neatly characterized. The natural sciences, the School of Practical Sciences, and the Banting Institute also find a place in this portrait of the University.

As preparation for this labor of love Callaghan talked to professors and students. His up-to-date impressions from such sessions are blended with nostalgic memories of his own college days. The names of several professors are mentioned with fond recollections. There are glimpses of rugby games, concerts, convocations, student discussions and debates, residential life, and visits to the Old Elm restaurant or the bootlegger Angelina. Most of these are made concrete in the associations of Warden Tyndall with fictionalized students. Callaghan uses one of these in particular, Tom Lane, as spokesman for his own ideas about education. Tom is an aspiring writer who believes in free time to browse, and who reads omnivorously and exuberantly. He refuses to apply for a

Rhodes scholarship "because the grandeurs and beauties of Oxford" might seduce him:

"All a writer has, if he is any good, . . . is his own eyes and his own ears, . . . I see things the way I do because I grew up around here. It's all I have, but it's mine. If I keep it I'll at least be trying to look at the world in my own way." [9]

Throughout *The Varsity Story* are sprinkled such remarks and attitudes which carry the unmistakable impression of Callaghan's own outlook. Viewed as a novel, the book has serious defects: its structure is loose and rambling; the time sequence is confusing; there is a plethora of historical and explanatory detail barely held together by the unifying character and quest of Tyndall; there is virtually no conflict of wills, climax or suspense to engage the reader; the other characters, who appear and disappear episodically, are manipulated like dummies by a ventriloquist; and the pragmatic hints to wealthy alumni regarding the need for extension of library and residence facilities detract from an already thin narrative. For graduates of Toronto and students of Callaghan's own earlier days, however, this "novel approach" with its evocative handling of mood and atmosphere holds the same nostalgic appeal which a fresh look at his alma mater quite evidently had for the author.

CHAPTER 7

The Two Worlds

IN AN illuminating study of Morley Callaghan's development as a novelist Professor Hugo McPherson examines Callaghan's vision of life:

At length . . . he has wrought out a fictional form in which the surface events function simultaneously as realistic action and symbolic action, revealing both the empirical and the spiritual conflicts of his protagonists. This duality, moreover, is never merely a tricky fictional device calculated to entertain both the naïve and the knowing; it is fundamental to Callaghan's perception of the interdependence of the spiritual and empirical realms. Man's career occurs in the imperfect world of time, but its meaning (man's dignity or "place") depends finally on a larger reality *out of time*. To escape the first world is physical death: to ignore the second is to embrace the condition of the Wasteland-life-in-death. This tension, to which Callaghan's best fiction gives dramatic form, is the fundamental tension of life. By exploring the relation of these two worlds—empirical and spiritual—Callaghan has written the "little man's" *Ash Wednesday* and *Burnt Norton*.[1]

Such Is My Beloved (1934), *They Shall Inherit The Earth* (1935) and *More Joy in Heaven* (1937) all clearly reflect this concept. It is even more evident in Callaghan's next two novels.

The Loved and The Lost (1951) and *The Many Colored Coat* (1960) are both set in Montreal. In his role as "counsel of the people" in the CBC program "Citizen's Forum" Callaghan often visited Montreal and came to know and appreciate its cosmopolitan charm. Situated on an island, it is a city of strong contrasts. Even to a tourist its geographical and sociological features— mountain and river, feudal French architecture and modern buildings, and its sharp division of population by districts as well as by its two cultures—are full of rich symbolic suggestion of man's isolation and conflict. For a novelist already preoccupied with the ironic tension between the values of two worlds, Montreal presents an irresistible setting.

I *The Loved and The Lost* (1951)

The Loved and The Lost, which Callaghan began writing as early as 1948, treats a complex theme. It presents again the dilemma of human weakness, of reconciling what man is with what he should be. It illustrates also that the attempt to live by one's own secret intuitions and to disregard social conventions can end only in frustration and tragedy—even when those secret intuitions are based on the spiritual values by which man should live. Yet in the novel somehow love also triumphs although all may seem lost.

The exposition and conflict are swiftly outlined. Jim McAlpine, associate professor of history at the University of Toronto, following the appearance of his article "The Independent Man" in the *Atlantic Monthly,* is invited to a January interview for a position as political columnist. His prospective employer, Joseph Carver, wealthy publisher of the Montreal *Sun,* is impressed by McAlpine's lively, authoritative style and by his quiet self-assurance. Carver's divorced daughter Catherine also approves of this handsome ex-naval officer from World War II with his dignified bearing and cultural interests. Jim, indeed, seems on the point of realizing the financial security and social status which have been his life-long ambition. Then he meets Peggy Sanderson, whose serene innocence and calm indifference to public opinion challenge his worldly values. Torn in his choice between the differing qualities which Catherine and Peggy represent, Jim, in his confusion of values, deserts Peggy at the crucial moment and thus shares a responsibility for her rape and murder by an unknown assailant.

The narrative of *The Loved and The Lost* advances with smooth precision and carefully managed suspense to its surprising yet logical dénouement. Presented primarily through the perceptions of McAlpine (although occasionally Carver or his daughter is the reader's sensorium), each episode is carefully foreshadowed. Central to the structure is Callaghan's characteristically skilful use of symbolism and irony. The setting itself provides a suggestive backdrop for the action. The mountain with the massive homes of the rich and its illuminated cross represents security and stability but also aspiration. The river with its slum districts and heterogeneous population represents flux: "Those who wanted things to remain as they were liked the mountain. Those who wanted a change preferred the broad flowing river." [2]

The duality introduced by the setting is continued in the symbolism employed in the characterization of the hero and heroine. Both Jim and Peggy have had a childhood experience which has had a profound effect in shaping their individual temperaments into Dostoevskian polarities: self-willed and agressive on the one hand, meek and self-renouncing on the other. Jim McAlpine's exclusion, at the age of fourteen, from a summer party of the wealthy Havelocks had crystallized in him a desire to climb (as his name suggests) to worldly success. Peggy Sanderson's secret view, at the age of twelve, of the naked colored boy, Jock Johnson, and her introduction to the happy companionship of his family had aroused in her a love and concern for the Negro race which irritate (as her name suggests) conventional society. Ironically, although Peggy, in the Café St. Antoine, and Jim, in the social circle of the Carvers, both join temporarily the different worlds from which they have been excluded in childhood, they do so as outsiders still who do not really belong.

Callaghan's development of Peggy's character is complex. College-educated daughter of a Methodist minister, she is a girl of beauty and mystery. Often Christ-like in her image, she has a baffling serenity, a warm affection for the poor and the outcast, and a reliance on her own "whirling-away feeling" of right. She is differently assessed or misunderstood by various people. To Jim she is like Saint Joan who "lived and acted by her own secret intuitions. Joan had shattered her world, and Peggy. . . . would shatter all the people who lived on the mountain and the people who prayed on the mountain." [3] By Chuck Foley, McAlpine's advertising executive friend, she is eventually considered "a big lie." To the satirical cartoonist Claude Gagnon and the embittered journalist Walter Malone her association with Negroes seems to be prompted by the crudest motives. By the coarse photographer Milton Rogers her attitude is described as ignorant, despicable "kissing the leper stuff." To the philosophical bartender Wolgast she is simply a frustrated seeker of the limelight. Even the Negro bandleader Elton Wagstaffe and his trumpet player Ronnie Wilson, who have been warmed by the glow of her affection, distrust her motivation and feel that she can only bring trouble to their people. Throughout the narrative Jim himself is in a torment of doubt concerning her real innocence. Nor does the reader have any certainty about her purity. She does, however, die resisting evil and her end is Christ-like: she is finally rejected in scorn by those she would befriend; she is denied, betrayed and forsaken by her loved one to suffer alone a humiliating death; her spirit returns to comfort Jim as he wanders forlornly about the streets looking vainly for the little old church that she had shown him on their first walk together.

Along with this mingling of Christian legend and medieval chronicle, Callaghan, by linking her to Eurydice of classical myth, adds overtones of meaning which universalize the haunting enigma of Peggy's character. When Jim defends her interest in Negroes to his friends at the Chalet Restaurant's Earbenders Club his remarks are cynically received.

"He makes speeches like music," Gagnon said finally. "Beautiful speeches in a pleasant tone. The right kind of music for Peggy. You follow me? There she is, lost in the dark underworld. Montreal's Plutonian shore. Like Eurydice. Remember the lady? Remember? How did Eurydice die?"

"Bitten by a snake," Foley said.

"And certainly our little Peggy has been badly bitten."

"So McAlpine becomes her Orpheus." [4]

Like Orpheus, Jim by his moment of doubt loses his beloved.

The old church to which Peggy takes Jim is a symbol of genuine Christian love. Actually seen only once by him, with its lines "half Gothic and half Romanesque, but light and simple in balance" framed against a white background of gently falling snow, it comes to represent the essential church of brotherhood whose bells are heard from afar and whose message is proclaimed in the spirit and conduct of Peggy. Viewed on the same day as this magical church of love is its counterpart, the contrasting symbol of violence, as represented in "a woodcarving of a leopard about three feet long in a glass case, crouching, ready to spring." [5] In her rapt contemplation of the carved (after Carver?) animal's jungle fierceness—a fascination which Jim ironically misinterprets later as a perverse attraction to violence—Peggy feels "uncertain and watchful" as though "waiting for the beast to spring at her." Like the black eye which she suffers in a disagreement with her lame artist friend Henry Jackson, this symbol vividly foreshadows the unleashed fury of the café brawl and the final tragic struggle of Peggy against her violator.

The black spots of the leopard and the white snowflakes falling on the quaint church as well as on Peggy's blonde hair suggest an antithesis of color which occurs throughout the novel. The mountain, home of the wealthy and influential white people, looms "like a dark protective barrier behind a shimmering curtain of lights surmounted by a gleaming cross." The square in the Negro section of the lower town near the Café St. Antoine is "all white with snow." These contrasting descriptive details, which accurately portray Montreal in winter, serve also to underline the dichotomy of good and evil and to intimate the conflicts characteristic of racial distinction.

The same kind of imagery is employed in three other individually developed symbols which add depth and meaning to the novel's basic conflict. The first of these is offered by McAlpine when he likens Peggy's initial impact on him to a wartime experience in Paris shortly after its liberation. On a dark and rainy evening along with an English officer McAlpine had discovered an "oasis of happiness" just off a dark alley:

"Then a door opened and we stepped into bright lights. Well, it was a little amphitheatre with the benches filled with people, and there was a tanbark surface and an encircling fence painted white, and down there in the toy arena were a couple of clowns in their pirouette costumes dancing around; a girl in a silver dress was riding a white horse; some one was leading an elephant across the arena. All this going on down there under a brilliant white light! Everything was so white and clean and fantastically surprising and so wonderfully innocent and happy. Maybe it looked like that because we had come in out of the darkness and the rain. We had come in out of the war. And the bright little circus was absolutely remote from the war. I was so surprised I gaped and blinked. It was beautiful. I felt so peacefully elated." [6]

Another occasion in which contrasts of color figure prominently is the episode in the Montreal Forum during a hockey game between the Rangers and the Canadiens. Surrounded by an audience drawn from various classes as well as races—English and French Canadians, American, Jewish and Negro—the teams perform in "a pretty pattern . . . just like the ballet." Yet when one of the players goes unpunished for an offense, the heterogeneous crowd is united in wild anger:

The ice was now a small white space at the bottom of a great black pit where sacrificial figures writhed, and on the vast slopes of the pit a maniacal white-faced mob shrieked at the one with the innocent air who had broken the rules, and the one who tolerated the offence. It was a yapping frenzied roaring.[7]

For McAlpine the mob scene provides a shocking parallel to Peggy's predicament. "Anything that breaks the pattern is bad. And Peggy breaks up the pattern." The only difference is that he feels "sure Peggy's innocent."

In explaining his antipathy to Peggy's introduction of a Negro into the Chalet Restaurant, its half-owner Wolgast relates a parable of his own ambition. As a child in Poland he had admired and loved a fine white horse driven by his father but owned by the landlord:

In the poverty-stricken life of a small boy, that white horse was a magic horse, able to carry him to places that were gay and free. It was like nothing else he had ever known. It got so that he was the only one who ever looked after the white horse. He came to believe it belonged to him.[8]

When his father was ordered to sell the horse, the boy had been desolate. Encouraged by his father's dying words, Wolgast resolved then that someday he would possess a white horse of his own. For him the Chalet is the realization of a dream which he does not want spoiled: he is determined to keep his own horse white.

This same image of men's individual ambitions recurs at the end of the book as Jim, trudging at dawn through the streets of melting snow, broods over his loss of Peggy:

When I knew I had her and could keep her, maybe I remembered that I too had come to Montreal to ride a white horse. Maybe that was why I was always trying to change her. That was the sin. I couldn't accept her as she was.[9]

Then as the sun touches the mountain top he has a sudden wild fancy:

the streets on the slopes of the mountain were echoing to the pounding of horses' hoofs. All the proud men on their white horses came storming down the slope of the mountain in a ruthless cavalry charge, the white horses whirling and snorting in the snow. And Peggy was on foot in the snow. She didn't own a white horse. She didn't want to. She didn't care. And he was beside her; but he drew back out of the way of the terrifying hoofs and they rode over her.

The device of contrast is effectively used also in the characterization. The circle of drinking companions of the Earbenders Club represents a different world from the group of Negroes who gather at the Café St. Antoine. Although the whites can visit the Negro district as tourists, the introduction of a colored person into Wolgast's bar brings a threat of violence against anyone who subsequently makes a similar breach of decorum. Peggy's world of factory hands, Negro porters and shoe-shine operators is juxtaposed with the comfortable, urbane society of the Carvers and the inveterate hostess Angela Murdock. The sharp antithesis between these milieux is essentially defined in the differently entitled sketches which McAlpine makes of Peggy and Catherine: "Peggy, the Crimper" and "Madame Radio."

Callaghan's psychological perceptiveness, his restraint and sure sense of dialogue in this novel bring all the various characters to life. Their different temperaments and dilemmas are probed and delineated with depth and power. Even peripheral figures like the shrewd detective Bouchard, who is somehow reminiscent of Dostoevsky's Porfiry in *Crime and Punishment,* emerge as individuals. His understanding of Catherine's resentment against McAlpine is as intuitive as his philosophical remark concerning Peggy's unknown murderer: "What if we all did it? The human condition. That has truth."

The central figures in the emotional triangle are especially vital. The portrayal of Catherine Carver is subtle and sympathetic. A beautiful divorcée, she is lonely and shy because of the secret knowledge that her possessiveness and desire to reform alienate men. Eager and generous in her impulses, she is always losing what she really wants. Her compassionate understanding of McAlpine's love for Peggy is affecting in its nobility:

> . . . the story of his devotion had filled her with sad regret that she herself had never stirred him, and yet she understood with generosity. A feverish glow was in her eyes as she listened. He's what I thought he was, she told herself. Loving and passionate and reckless and impulsive and faithful. No wonder I loved him.[10]

Listening to his confession at the police station, she shares vicariously her rival's emotions and thoughts. Peggy's betrayal by McAlpine becomes Catherine's own betrayal. The blending of the attitudes of the two opposing female characters makes Catherine's savage rebuke to him tantamount to an expression of censure by all womanhood.

Although the ambiguity of Peggy's personality teases the reader, she is made plausible by such human weaknesses as untidiness and an attitude that is frequently deliberately provocative, as well as by her admission of "the failure of her judgment of herself and others." Peggy's warm and spontaneous friendliness (as undiscriminating as that of Browning's "My Last Duchess") and her inscrutable nature, moreover, make believable Jim's fascination, tortured misunderstanding and climactic betrayal.

The novel is rich in its light-handed satire of business, academic life, social prejudices, mob hysteria and orthodox religion. Joseph Carver applauds independence but ironically crushes it in his treatment of his own employees. As a university governor he is contemptuous of professors. Expediency and prudent conformity are the qualities which Jim must learn if he wants to take his place in the *Sun* and really belong inside the high dark hedges which enclose the domains of the wealthy. Beneath the surface veneer of civilization there are always lurking the jungle fury and demoniac frenzy of mob hysteria, which can break out suddenly in a hockey scuffle or a café riot. Peggy's father, who has lost his faith as a

Methodist minister under the wordly pressures of an urban church, cannot support his daughter in her attempt to practise unreservedly the doctrine of love. Nor does McAlpine imagine that a priest would be any more helpful:

Get her into a confessional with him: "I confess to the Almighty God and to thee, father. I confess to having no sense of discrimination. I confess to not keeping my love for the right ones. I confess to bringing out the worst in people and turning one man against another. Why do I bring no peace to anybody, father?" . . . "My dear child, it's complicated. You must not be a nuisance. Guard yourself against the opinion that those who stand for law and order are always at war with those who stand for—well, this uncontrolled tenderness and goodness of yours. Examine it carefully, my dear child, in the light of the greater harmony. St. Augustine would say—" [11]

The appeal of *The Loved and The Lost* is varied and enduring. It won the Governor-General's Award for Fiction in 1951 and has since become a prescribed study in university courses on Canadian literature. It has demonstrated its popular as well as academic success by the sale of over half a million copies in an inexpensive paperback edition. In 1955 it was adapted as a Broadway musical, with Albert Moritz writing the music and Thomas Chastain the lyrics. Elaborate costs of production and lack of financial backing, however, prevented its presentation. The absorbing theme, suspenseful action, careful interweaving of detail, illuminating symbolic structure, ironical distortion, realistic characterization, and haunting pathos make *The Loved and The Lost* an arresting and memorable novel.

II   *The Many Colored Coat* (1960)

As early as 1953 Callaghan began another novel obviously set in Montreal—although that city's name is not specifically mentioned —which in its time span of summer and autumn completes the seasonal cycle begun in *The Loved and The Lost*. The first version of this new book, entitled *The Man With The Coat*, won a five thousand dollar award from *Maclean's* and appeared in an abridged form in that magazine's issue of April 16, 1955. Out of this original work grew the full length novel *The Many Colored*

Coat, a dramatic and penetrating examination of innocence, guilt and conscience in modern society.

Harry Lane, handsome and charming public relations director for a large distillery, by his amiable generosity attracts into the dazzling glamour of his circle a middle-aged banker, Scotty Bowman. When a grateful friend gives Harry a present of some shares in an apparently promising oil venture, he is urged by Scotty to capitalize on this inside information and purchase more stock by borrowing from his bank. In return for negotiating what appears to Harry to be a legitimate loan, Scotty slyly suggests that he be given a share of the oil stock. The investment proves worthless. Scotty is convicted of fraud and sent to prison where he commits suicide. The trial, at which Harry is silent about his friend's avaricious complicity, and Scotty's cowardly death ironically bring public opprobrium on the legally innocent Harry. After fruitless attempts to convince people of his blamelessness, he begins to wear constantly a tropical suit made by a protégé of Scotty, Mike Kon, whose testimony at the trial had made Scotty look like the victim of a slick charmer. For Harry, this suit, which has a defective lining, becomes the symbol of truth for all the world to see.

As the title intimates, the hero's career bears a relation to that of the Biblical Joseph. Harry is envied for his favored and prosperous position in society. He is falsely maligned, suffers ignominy, eventually forgives those who have wronged him and is finally completely exonerated. He also has significant dreams, and a coat plays an important part in his change of fortune. Except for these obvious similarities, however, and the implied point of view that "nothing evil could happen to a good man," the Old Testament parallel is not closely followed. In some ways the coat actually resembles the glove thrown down in a medieval challenge to a duel of honor.[12] "Many-colored" as an epithet, moreover, represents the many aspects which this jacket eventually comes to symbolize. As its tailor, Mike is guilty of *hubris;* despite his pride of workmanship, the coat's attractive exterior conceals an interior rottenness. Like his courtroom evidence, and indeed like Scotty's character and reputation, the cloth has hidden flaws: it lacks integrity. "Many-colored" suggests Harry's initial "popularity, his charm, his easy superiority";[13] it also signifies his legal innocence, moral unawareness, self-righteousness, pride, stubbornness, ultimate recognition of a share of responsibility in Scotty's death, and conviction that personal reconciliation is more important than public acquittal.

In his structural technique Callaghan moves with ease and confidence. The exposition swiftly introduces Scotty through whose perceptions the two central figures are initially presented. His shrewd and likable temperament and his middle position as admired friend of Mike and wistful admirer of Harry are carefully delineated. The oil stock deal and its sequel provide the generating circumstances that cause the latent tension between protagonist and antagonist to erupt openly. The first trial spells out clearly the basic image which runs throughout the novel: like the balancing courtroom scene at the conclusion, it dramatizes the idea that life itself is a trial. This continual sifting of weighty moral values is kept vital and absorbing by a suspenseful action which moves forward largely through the lively dialogue of the characters. The courtroom scenes, which reflect Callaghan's own legal training, are particularly compelling in their realistic interchange of question and answer.

The employment of a triad of main characters with supporting triangular relationships built around the hero and his girl (here involving Scotty, Judge and Mrs. Morris, the parents of Mollie, and her rival Annie Laurie) and the suggestive use of the numeral three are typical of Callaghan's work. In *The Many Colored Coat,* however, a binary rather than a triangular pattern predominates. Even though after his death Scotty's personality continues to have a malignantly catalytic effect on Harry and Mike, these two alone dominate the stage. Their continuing duel and progress towards complete self-vindication are plotted inversely along curiously parallel lines. At the time of Scotty's indictment they are both successful business executives who move in overlapping circles of mutual friends or acquaintances. These circles are neatly assembled at Scotty's trial in which Harry and Mike are both called as witnesses. Under the questioning of prosecutor Henderson and especially of lawyer Ouimet, however, Harry is virtually put on trial himself. Mike's incriminating evidence intensifies the impression that Harry has taken advantage of a friendship. Henceforth each progresses independently, though in different sequence, through a series of similar experiences upon which the other has a

constant influence. For Harry the succession is enraged humiliation and loss of position, friends and confidence. He reaches the
nadir of this descending Dantesque cycle when Mike refuses to
repair the defective coat lining: "It was then Harry started wearing the light tropical suit." [14] From this pivotal point the fortunes
of Mike and Harry startlingly reverse their flows. The latter now
enjoys a growing sense of personal dignity and public approval
while Mike begins to suffer mortification, rejection and financial
loss. Like Harry, he seeks a solution to his dilemma by a visit to
lawyer Ouimet. Mike's own request to repair Harry's coat is denied, and his uncontrollable rage eventually brings him into court
again, ironically now in the role not of respected witness but of
accused prisoner. Finally, both protagonist and antagonist, after
their separate painful experiences of Inferno and Purgatory, individually attain a condition of relative innocence which, like that
of Dante's Eden, is purged of the deadly sin of pride.

These parallels emerge strikingly when excerpts of relevant dialogue are placed together. Harry wonders "could he sue Kon for
slander, for defamation of character?" just as Mike later explodes
"It's a campaign of slander. . . . I want to sue him." [15] As Harry
rejects Max Sweetman's advice, "Go to Florida, stay away till this
stupid little bank manager is forgotten," so Mike refuses to accept
a similar suggestion for a cooling-off period from his helper Willie:
"Look, why don't you take a little holiday? Go down to Miami." [16]
Discussing Harry's future with the distillery Max remarks, "My
God, man, you'd be a target. It's impossible." Singerman, Mike's
silent partner, likewise warns him, "With a bad reputation, you're
no good to me." [17] Both opponents cry out for understanding:
Harry's "Pay attention to me. . . . I've lived my life here. . . .
Pay attention to me about that man" is echoed by Mike's "Pay
attention to me, you hear. Have some respect for a man." [18] These
examples of their own similar comments could be multiplied. The
response of each's circle of friends forms a similarly parallel pattern: they grow silent and embarrassed [19] by the intensity first of
Harry's, and then of Mike's hatred.[20] Both men in turn quarrel
with their girls and try to find solace in liquor because they feel
uneasy in their old haunts.

The public resolution of this struggle in the common police
court, presided over by "a beery little magistrate" rather than a

distinguished judge, brings together again all the significant figures except Harry and, of course, Scotty. Mollie Morris, giving evidence in a final gesture of loyalty to Harry, ironically experiences the same humiliating treatment under the clever cross-examination of defense lawyer Ouimet as Harry had suffered at the initial trial. Warm-hearted and lovely Annie Laurie, advertising executive Ted Ogilvie, bank superintendent Slocombe, sports editor Haggerty, dignified steak house proprietor Alfred Dorfman and prosecutor Henderson—"in fact whole rows of the self-same faces"—appear before Mike's eyes. This repetition with variation of the earlier episode in which innocence and guilt are formally examined in a court of justice neatly underlines the main theme. The conclusion, moreover, is an ironical commentary on the superiority of enlightened individual conscience over conventional social judgment.

Good-natured social satire helps to lighten the novel's dominating mood of intense conflict. The hollow world of commercial advertising and public relations forms an amusing as well as effective contrast with the sincerity of Harry and Mike. Mollie's wealthy neighborhood is characterized by "a kind of English accent that had been gained twenty-five years ago when it had been the fashion to import English nannies for the nursery, although most of these nannies had cockney accents which the children had then picked up and smoothed out." [21] Similarly, in court "two matrons from Westmount, walking up and down gossiped in English accents that didn't come from England." Chauffeur-gardener Green, trailing "after Mrs. Morris in the chain stores, carrying her basket" and respectfully disregarding the Judge's opinion on the proper care of rose bushes, senile Joseph Marston, who "had taken to going out to the front lawn and wetting in the moonlight," anxious Dr. Henshaw, "waiting for his delinquent fifteen-year-old daughter," brilliant and decorative committee wives with their tired, graying husbands, Dorfman's, "old expensive restaurant catering to the elite," mediocre writers hungry for public acclaim and even the priest obsessed with the sins of the flesh all present a searching yet comically ironic cross-section of modern affluent society.

Irony, of course, is everywhere. Harry's dilemma is a mockery of his position as a public relations director. As Esther Sweetman bluntly remarks with a Falstaffian echo: "Honor won't put money in the bank, sell whiskey, or buy one of your twenty-five dollar shirts." [22] The entire trial is an ironical misrepresentation of the actual facts. Scotty's real motive of avarice is summarily dismissed as unthinkable and his shrewd ability to assess clients is used to strengthen his image as an injured party. Paradoxically, however, this is the trait which continues to plague Mike's conscience until he reverses his earlier position and becomes Harry's advocate. Scotty's funeral service is a travesty as the minister confidently speaks of "a man of such established integrity that when he had been blinded and turned in another direction, it had been so alien to his whole life and character he had been driven out of his mind. Considering that he knew nothing about Scotty or Harry, it was a moving tribute." [23] Mike's prophecy that he will make "a suit I'll be proud to have you wear, Harry" is as ironically contradicted as are Harry's own aspirations and plans for self-vindication.

Although the underlying symbolism of *The Many Colored Coat* is less obtrusive than in previous novels, there are a number of images which contribute to the significance of particular actions or to the atmosphere. When Mollie fails in her attempt to share Harry's terrifying guiltlessness by a complete physical surrender, the moment is marked by background sounds of childhood's less calculated innocence and a convent's dedicated innocence: "the nuns under the pear tree in the garden laughing and chattering brightly . . . and the sound of the bouncing rubber ball, the little girl trying to catch it in her cupped hand." [24] Her coverage of a newspaper story of a cowardly teen-ager who allowed his girl to be raped arouses a suggestive response in Mollie. As she watches the comforting embrace given to the unheroic boy, she wonders "if the destruction of all dignity and respect could come from love as well as hate," whether she was both harboring and destroying Harry.[25] The image of lions and tigers occurs frequently. Harry is described as "a raging lion" and Mike gains the soubriquet of "Tiger" as they continue their savage feud. There are frequent squalls and periods of cloud. Sometimes, as the sun tries to break through, various characters shield their eyes from these penetrating rays.

Two other episodes provide illuminating parallels to Harry's predicament. The first of these describes the comeback of a night club singer Denise La Coste (whose predicament contains the germ of Callaghan's later novel *A Passion in Rome*). At one time internationally famous, she suffered a serious breakdown. On her first attempt to sing again in public she forgot the lyrics; on the second occasion, her success is overwhelming. As the audience applauds her performance, Harry spontaneously rises to invite her to his table in a gesture which is misinterpreted as a bid for attention. This "comic relief" curiously links his position in the reader's mind with that of the singer. Even though it casts Harry in a burlesque part, it also augurs for him a successful rehabilitation and public approval.

Similarly the middleweight championship bout between the bull-shouldered Flying Dutchman and his more agile opponent Johnny Bruno under the white focus of spotlights is a prefiguration of the fight between Mike and Harry which takes place in Dorfman's restaurant. This formalized image of the duel can also be interpreted as a prelude to the final scene in court where first Mike, and then Harry, in a reversal of obvious roles, emerge like the Flying Dutchman winners by default.

The commanding figures involved in this struggle for a true perspective are drawn with particular richness. It is, indeed, Callaghan's psychological insight and consistency and the realistic way in which he develops their complexity that make plausible what might otherwise seem an absurdly unrealistic burlesque. Harry Lane's background is quickly presented. Son of a socially respected family, he had interrupted a medical course to enlist in the air force during World War II. After the sudden death of both his parents within a year of his return from five years overseas service, he had been offered a lucrative position by Max Sweetman:

At first Harry had felt a little ashamed of himself, cultivating good will for the distillery with all the Sweetman money behind him. Harry had always been honest in all his feelings about people. Now he felt he was developing a false relationship with the whole world. He started to drink heavily. Once, he disappeared for three days. Sweetman found him holed up in a bordello drunkenly happy, reading the plays of Shakespeare to the girls. Harry did these foolish things because it went against his grain to be consciously putting himself in a good light, always doing complimentary things for people. But he wasn't aware yet that the job, with all the money it gave him to spend, was gradually appealing to a quality in him that was inseparably honest and attractive. He had always had a talent for generosity.[26]

Partly because this generosity is cynically interpreted as motivated by business reasons he feels the need of "a simple solid honest friendship of an older man like Scotty Bowman." The shrewd banker also feels strangely drawn to this affable friend and wonders about the secret of his charm:

What was that astonishing air of well-being which seemed to suggest that all the phonies in the world could come against Harry Lane and he would shame them because he knew that nothing evil could happen to a good man? Was that it? A naïve man? A man of simple good feeling under the glad-hand role? [27]

In his relationship with his fiancée, Judge Morris' beautiful and virginal daughter Mollie, Harry finds another touchstone of that integrity to which his own nature responds sympathetically.

The very virtues of his personality ironically precipitate his dilemma. It is Scotty who appropriately diagnoses Harry's "bad flaw. He's a kind of innocent guy." [28] His plight is actually universalized in its overtones. To Mollie he sounds "like an ancient Greek hero" as he calmly explains that "his big mistake . . . was in violating his nature in not telling the whole truth." [29] He is also described as "quixotic" in his role of righter of wrongs. Like a classical tragic figure and Don Quixote, too, he is finally compelled to examine his own actions, motives and conscience. This crucial period of self-analysis begins in a nightmarish scene following a confession to an apparently foolish but paradoxically wise priest:

Harry had never had any desire to get outside his own life, or even thought about such matters. Until the trial he had been too comfortable. It had been his vocation to make other people comfortable with a handshake and a few words on a street corner, or at his big parties to which he invited everybody. Just naturally he had played ball with people without any real sense of duplicity, just a little good-humored cynicism here and there.[30]

The attempt to be honest with himself repeatedly challenges his stubborn determination to vindicate himself by hounding the tailor into court again. Even while playing this stalking role he instinctively longs for an honorable reconciliation with Mike. Harry's open door in the rooming house to which he moves suggests that he has never "really cut himself off from the world." [31] Nor does his provocation of Mike's savage assault and the knowledge that the witness will now become the accused bring Harry the satisfaction that he has anticipated. Lying in the hospital bed and later pacing his own room, he is tormented by his conscience and the realization that "innocence was like a two-edged sword without a handle, and if you gripped it and used it, it cut you so painfully you had to lash out blindly, seeking vengeance on someone for the bleeding." [32] His new awareness prompts Harry to reject the cheap prospect of "a comeback triumph in court in the jailing of Mike Kon" and to turn instead toward "a new world of new relationships with people." This entire presentation of Harry's internal struggle illustrates Callaghan's ability to convey a complex moral idea in a humanly understandable metaphor that is yet aphoristic.

Although contrasting physically and temperamentally, Harry and Mike are united in their common humanity. Brought up in the tough East End, Mike became a middleweight fighter. After retiring from the ring because of an eye injury, he has become proprietor of a successful clothing store started with financial backing arranged by Scotty. His wide reading, his colorful language and exciting recollections of boxing experiences have gained him the name of "Mike the Scholar." To this simple, loyal friend, so familiar with the rigged deals of sport, it appears obvious that Scotty has been seduced by Harry's charm. The latter's campaign to destroy Mike's cherished respectability, moreover, seems like an attack on justice itself. The stages in his ordeal are subtly foreshadowed and its end is intimated in Harry's bitter pun on the name Kon, "Konscience." Only when Mike confesses in the public courtroom that he was wrong to judge, to accuse Harry out of blind friendship for Scotty, does he regain a sense of honest self-respect.

Callaghan's delineation of Scotty Bowman is particularly deft. From it springs the dilemma of protagonist and antagonist. Apparently happily married, father of two teen-age sons, Scotty is a respected bank manager. His outside interests appear plebeian and harmless. Yet beneath his solid exterior and shrewdly appraising eyes lurk romantic yearnings. His association with Mike at frequent fights has encouraged his desire for a more exciting life than that provided by "his dull bridge-playing neighbors." In Harry Lane's ease, luck and success, Scotty sees crystallized all his own day-dreams. Dazzled into believing that some of these qualities would rub off on him, he plunges into the oil gamble. Just as he relies on Harry's generosity after the loan to let him take over five thousand shares of stock, so when his arrest is imminent Scotty appeals to this same generosity to conceal the incriminating participation. At the time of the trial his human weakness is delicately conveyed. In spite of a sense of shame that his silence should impugn his friend's reputation, for the sake of his own family he wants the consolation of being seen in the most sympathetic light. This desire is reinforced by his rationalization:

Why did you come into the bank that day and give me the tickets to the fight, Harry? he thought bitterly. Answer me that, Harry? Why didn't you leave me alone? If you hadn't given me those tickets I wouldn't be here and you know it. With this bitter cry in his heart he could resist Harry's proud contempt.[33]

Scotty's final desperate act of suicide ironically completes his public image as "the wronged ruined man." The portrayal is affecting and effective because of Callaghan's artistic integrity: he does not give the reader a wilfully disingenuous schemer, but a believable man whose feelings make his actions understandable.

Two other characters play sufficiently significant and contrasting roles to merit brief attention. They are the women who share Harry's traumatic experience. Beautiful brunette Mollie Morris, only daughter of respectable but emotionally shrivelled parents, who writes for the Women's Page of the *Sun*, genuinely tries to remain loyal to Harry. Yet she cannot leave behind her own comfortable world. Her plight is graphically described in an image repeated from "In His Own Country." Harry's maternal grandparents

had come out to the ship on the tender with twenty other emigrants to the new world. Then they had stood at the ship's rail looking back at the land they had loved and they had been full of tears, and some of the men had been singing and some of the women wailing. Harry's great-grandfather and his wife had got separated and he hadn't worried about her until the ship had sailed. Then he couldn't find her. Later one of the crew had told him he had seen a woman passenger making her way back to the small boat and being taken aboard. Her husband knew she couldn't bear to leave the land she loved and had gone back. It would happen with Mollie, Harry thought.[34]

Blonde and lovely Annie Laurie MacNiece, on the other hand, has "none of Mollie's lofty self-regard" and is warm-heartedly indifferent to the world's conventions or opinions. Despite her easy virtue she has freshness and spontaneity. She is, in fact, almost too charming to be plausible. While Mollie leaves Harry alone in his time of trial to go off to the cottage with her parents, Annie with unquestioning faith generously looks after him. In the relations between these two women there is an underlying counterpart to the duel of the main plot. Although both have been schooled in the social graces, their worlds are widely separated. Mollie, a slave to her heritage and environment, is too weak to confront her rival in the street: "She dreaded the look she might get from Annie, the amused pitying smile coming out of the pretty woman's secret cynical knowledge of love and its satisfaction." [35] In Mollie's jealous rationalization, Harry's association with Annie is an indication of "how low he had fallen." During the last courtroom scene where both women are witnesses, Annie's wise understanding of the conflict contrasts with Mollie's unwittingly damaging testimony. The final blow to pride of respectability is Annie's simple gesture of genuine sympathy for Mollie's humiliation.

Around these five central figures moves a number of minor characters into whose thoughts and feelings the reader is given perceptive glimpses. Some of these people are appropriately arranged in pairs and are involved between themselves in overt or latent conflicts which erupt in their differing opinions about Harry. Judge and Mrs. Morris both pass resentful judgment on him because his warm charm—"his disgusting bedroom sense of intimacy"—reminds them of their own failure to achieve an intimate marital relationship. Yet Helena Morris, in spite of herself, is drawn to Harry's sympathetic nature. Gentle Max Sweetman, at the insistence of his insensitive, social-climbing wife Esther, reluctantly drops Harry; but Max quarrels with Esther because he intuitively understands and appreciates Harry's nobility. In a similar way each of the other significant individual characters—Ouimet, Ogilvie, Haggerty, the boxing circle of Ray Conlin, and Harry's two wartime associates and grateful beneficiaries, McCance and Gorman—plays a direct part in probing essential questions of truth, guilt, innocence and justice.

Every individual has a different conception of these qualities and each one believes his own version of the truth. Harry sees at the trial that in reporting their own conversation "Mike had told the truth, word for word; only it isn't the truth, he thought desperately. It was only the truth as those imprudent thoughtless kidding words had revealed it to him." [36] These varying interpretations for Harry put "the whole world in false face. No one quite in the place he pretends to be." [37] In the same vein, Max Sweetman philosophically observes to him about Scotty, "The truth about any man is pretty hard to tell, because someone else always has another angle on him." [38] This platitude, as so often happens in Callaghan's writing, becomes meaningful in context.

The related problems of guilt, innocence and justice are equally thorny. Scotty is found legally guilty but is virtually exonerated by society. Harry is judged by society as morally guilty. Mike admits his own guilt in accusing Harry because of blind loyalty to Scotty. Judge Morris and Ouimet are both guilty of judging Harry not by professional legal standards but from the point of view of personal prejudice. He himself recognizes in his nightmare of personal cross-examination the kaleidoscopic nature of justice. Was his generosity and kindness to Scotty really selfishness and egotism? Is any "man supposed to act as policeman over the soul of another?" [39] Do not even the prudence and scruples of the Christian conscience separate man from man? The Tragedy of this failure in human relationships is poignantly presented in a chance street encounter between Mike and Harry:

They both wanted to speak, reach a peaceful settlement. But they were so far apart now that neither one trusted the first words he would have to use, or any words needed to tell what was in his heart; they shared for the moment that helpless angry feeling. There was no way of communicating, nor showing any recognition of what they felt almost furtively as a desperate need.[40]

[146]

One dangerous aspect of innocence, already touched on in Callaghan's treatment of the heroine of *The Loved and The Lost* and suggested by Scotty, is naïveté. As Harry on the night before the second trial ponders over his new insight into himself, he wonders whether unawareness is not "the greatest of sins. . . . by this sin fell the proudly innocent." [41] Like Peggy Sanderson, he, too, comes to recognize that "you can't go against people. . . . You can't try to embarrass the whole world and expect to get away with it." [42] For Peggy awareness had come only on the night of her death. In the magazine version *The Man With The Coat* Harry dies before he has reached this stage although Mike experiences a measure of it. In *The Many Colored Coat* Harry moves beyond naïveté towards "some awareness that could give width and depth to a man's whole life." [43]

The emphasis on the idea that the individual must work out his own salvation is consistent with Callaghan's concept of life: each man's own private conscience is the best guide to a satisfying existence. In the clash between the spiritual and empirical world, as Mike observes in a colorful comment reminiscent of *More Joy in Heaven*, "There's no such thing as a public conscience. It's one thing today, something else to-morrow. It's like an old piano. . . . Who's the player, that's all." [44] If *The Many Colored Coat* in its representation of Scotty's fate is a modern *exemplum* of the sage comment of Solon, "True blessedness consisteth in a good life and a happy death," it is also a dramatic reminder that innocence is a many-colored coat and "maybe no one has a right to take it for granted people are going to believe in him no matter what the situation is." [45]

III *Morley Callaghan's Stories* (1959)

Some of the tales in Callaghan's third collection, *Morley Callaghan's Stories*, also illustrate his interest in the way that individuals resolve the tension between empirical and spiritual values. Inscribed with affectionate nostalgia "To the way it has been with us," this book contains fifty-seven pieces. Of these, twelve had already appeared in *A Native Argosy* (1929) and thirty-two in *Now That April's Here* (1936). The remaining thirteen were written from 1936 through 1953. As a prologue to the collection Callaghan wrote:

Many other stories I have written might have been included in this book, but these are the ones that touch times and moods and people I like to remember now. Looking back on them I can see that I have been concerned with the problems of many kinds of people but I have neglected those of the very, very rich. I have a story that begins, "Once upon a time there were two millionaires," but I haven't finished it yet.

Four of the thirteen tales still to be discussed were reprinted in annual editions of O'Brien's *The Best Short Stories* from 1937 through 1941. "The Voyage Out," included in O'Brien's 1937 edition, depicts the intricate and powerful emotions of a young man in love. Walking home elated by the thought that his nice girl Jessie would have surrendered to him but for the fact that her parents were awake, Jeff stops at a restaurant for a cup of coffee. There the cynical remarks of the baker Mike that a respectable looking girl was really "a soft touch" make Jeff's warm glow of romantic yearning seem childish.

Back in his apartment he encounters his older brother's girl, Eva, waiting red-eyed and frightened for Bill. Although previously on easy companionable terms with her, Jeff now looks over Eva so shrewdly and sensually that she leaves in embarrassment and he is ashamed of his lascivious behavior. Later Bill, who is unemployed, admits that Eva is pregnant. Although this revelation that passion may result in misery shocks Jeff, his desire for Jessie soon dispels his fear of any such similar consequences. Life's irresistible rhythm is neatly conveyed in the last paragraph of this little Depression tableau of love's progress in which romantic yearning, sensual cynicism and harsh reality are neatly juxtaposed and eventually blended:

He got up restlessly, realizing that neither Mike's wisdom nor his brother's anguish could teach him anything tonight. Standing at the open window, he looked out over the lighted streets where he walked a little while ago, looking over toward Jessie's place, stirred with a longing for more and more of whatever she would be able to give him. It had started now for them and it would keep going on. And then he was filled with awe, for it seemed like the beginning of a voyage out, with not much he had learned on that night to guide him.

"The Cheat's Remorse," which was included in the 1938 edition of *The Best Short Stories,* is set in New York. Phil, needing money to pay for a clean shirt so that he can apply for a promised job, sees a prosperous drunk drop a dollar in a restaurant. Before Phil can pick up the bill, a pale-faced girl puts her foot on it. In a toss for the dollar he wins by using a phony coin. Full of remorse at the girl's stricken face, he attempts to give her the money. She refuses to accept it on the grounds that the price of a clean shirt may give him a new start but cannot really help her own position.

The incident is told with ironical poignancy. The prosperous looking, blue-jowled and fat drunk, with the roll of bills and untouched sandwich, contrasts with the lean and poorly dressed young people. Their mutual anxiety to get the dollar, the girl's eager "sigh, as if all the hope she ever had in her life was on the coin," her bravely concealed desperation and his feeling of shame over the rigged toss are precisely portrayed by terse dialogue and description. The conclusion captures not only the inexorable mood of despair which pervaded the Depression era but also the nobility and baseness of human nature.

She walked away resolutely this time, as if she had made some final destructive decision, a decision she had dreaded and that she mightn't have made if he hadn't cheated her and she had got the dollar.

Worried, he went to run after her, but he stopped, startled and shaken, perceiving the truth as she had seen it, that a dollar in the long run was no good to her, that it would need a vast upheaval that shook the earth to really change the structure of her life. Yet she had been willing to stop and help him.

But the clean shirt became an absurd and trivial thing and the dollar felt unclean in his hand. He looked down the street at the tavern light. He had to get rid of the dollar or feel that he'd always see her walking away resolutely with her hands deep in her pockets.

"It Had to be Done," included in the 1939 edition of *The Best Short Stories,* is set in the Delaware Valley. The story depicts the embarrassing necessity for a young woman Catherine to intervene in helping her fiancé break off permanently with a wealthy widow. As an aspiring but penniless architect Chris had become the protégé of Mrs. Mumford but had eventually left her when she tried to dominate his life. At her invitation he is returning to her country estate to pick up some suits she had once bought for him. Although he wished to go alone on this trip, Catherine insists on accompanying him. Waiting outside the big white house for some time she feels "suddenly lost in a country that belonged to a rich woman" and her mind is filled with doubts about her fiancé's love. Awkwardly interrupting the two, Catherine breaks the spell of the older woman and releases Chris' love for herself.

The story is a sensitive *aperçu* of a critical moment of conflict in a love triangle. Blonde, slim and attractive Catherine is fifteen years younger than her dark-haired, large and handsome rival. As the modest social and financial background of the one is set against the sophistication and opulence of the other, so also is Catherine's frank and even vulgar display of her physical superiority as a future wife contrasted with Mrs. Mumford's calculating and selfish possessiveness. Despite Chris' humiliation, his response to Catherine's rejection of Mrs. Mumford's proprietary claim on him is a vindication of his fiancée's earlier conviction that "it had to be done."

"Getting on in the World," included in *The Best Short Stories* edition of 1940, deftly portrays the ironic outcome of a foolish young man's warped sense of values. Henry Forbes, pianist in a hotel tavern, dreams of becoming successful by winning the approval of influential clients. Into his life comes an old friend's sister, Jean Gorman, young, eager and loving. Sitting beside him night after night as he plays the piano she is happy to share his company. About to lose his job unless someone puts in a good word for him, he persuades Jean to go alone to a party held by a corrupt political boss, Eddie Convey. Only after she has reluctantly agreed does Henry realize how he has betrayed her warm tenderness. When she finally comes out of Convey's apartment at four o'clock in the morning her fresh glow of innocence has been replaced by a knowing and self-satisfied air.

The very detachment with which this story is presented accentuates its tragi-comic incongruity. The conclusion, in which Henry's belated concern is rejected, neatly reverses the positions of the two central figures. Jean's hesitant and troubled mood as he persuades her to attend the party is recalled in his perturbed realization outside the apartment that he has really been a Pander; her impulsively warm kiss as she reluctantly goes to the party has its counterpart in the slap she gives him when they meet again afterwards. Finally, Henry's frustrated ambitions and his fruitless infatuation with the glamour of important clients are balanced by Jean's easy success and actual acceptance into their meretricious world.

"Watching and Waiting" is a melodramatic illustration that a husband too can be unperceptive and unappreciative of the warm tenderness of his wife. Tom Hilliard is so consumed with unreasoning distrust that even when he has turned back home with a sense of shame and yearning to comfort his wife after a spat he cannot control his jealousy. With ironic justice he is shot to death as a spying prowler by his innocent spouse.

"Magic Hat" and "Very Special Shoes" center around treasured possessions which appear to be spoiled and then unexpectedly bring the genuine pleasure of which they originally gave promise. In the former story, a Chinese coolie hat made with painstaking care, although drooping with wet snow, wins a proposal of marriage for a young woman about to be deserted. The experience illustrates that the course of people's lives can "change as the result of a little thing like an unpremeditated glance at a hat." "Very Special Shoes" depicts a poor little girl's longing for a pair of red leather shoes. After gaining the approval of her father and mother to purchase this luxury, Mary has no opportunity to try out the shoes before her mother dies during an operation for cancer. The shoes are dyed for the funeral and henceforth Mary wears them daily as a symbol of her mother's blessing:

Of course now that they were black they were not noticed by other children. But she was very careful with them. Every night she polished them up and looked at them and was touched again by that secret joy.

"The White Pony" and "A Cap for Steve" also treat symbols which represent youth's frustration and eventual growth to an awarenesss of life. Tony's love for a circus pony is exploited by its smiling red-haired trainer. Although the boy carries water, he is not allowed to caress or ride the pony. Angrily he realizes that he has been cheated,

that the big fellow had simply used him, that that was the kind of thing they took for granted in the world he had wanted to grow into when he had glimpsed it from the garage window.

In "A Cap for Steve" Callaghan demonstrates again his ability to portray, without being infantile or sentimental, the misunderstandings and emotional differences which separate a child's world from that of adults. Steve Diamond, shy son of a poor carpenter's assistant, is given a baseball cap by a famous Philly outfielder. This cap becomes a magic talisman which transforms Steve into a leader in the park. After losing the cap, he recognizes it in the possession of a wealthy lawyer's son. Steve is dismayed when his father agrees to sell it to its new owner for twenty dollars. Yet because both father and son in turn give up what they value most to each other and Mr. Diamond recognizes the inestimable worth of the cap to his son, there comes to the father an exalted yet humble feeling of "the wonderful generosity of childhood—the price a boy was willing to pay to be able to count on his father's admiration and approval."

In two other stories a boy is the central figure. The first of these, "The Little Business Man," is *The Saturday Evening Post* story from which Callaghan's juvenile novel *Luke Baldwin's Vow* was developed. The second, entitled "A Very Merry Christmas," is a charming tale in which an image of the infant Jesus disappears from its place in a church tableau of Bethlehem. The excited parish priest is certain that Communists or atheists are responsible; the godly old caretaker wonders quietly and is saddened by his sense of loss; the police and general public are puzzled about the motive for the apparent crime. The mystery is quickly solved. Little Jimmie Farrel admits that he got up early on Christmas Day to make good a promise which he made to "God that if He would make Mother bring me a big red sleigh for Christmas I would give Him the first ride on it." This simple expression of faith in the Christmas spirit and the child's joyous gesture of gratitude quietly rebuke the priest's angry suspicions, Jimmie's mother's outraged sense of decorum and the gravely formal disapproval of the parishioners.

"Their Mother's Purse" illustrates how little parents really know about their own children. When Joe savagely questions his younger sister about two dollars she has stolen from her mother's purse, he discovers that Mary is supporting a husband in a sanatorium. Impressed by her frightened, eager face, Joe promises to keep the secret. The incident brings home to him the realization of how easily and imperceptibly a family can drift apart.

The final story in this collection is full of poignancy. In "The Homing Pigeon" a seventeen-year-old youth, whose mother has recently died, sets out to bring home his alcoholic father. Driving into New York to check out an address which he has found on an envelope, Dick experiences "an indescribable elation, a puzzled breathlessness." He discovers his father, Dr. Harvey, with a blonde in a cheap boarding house. Shamed at the sight of this behavior, Dick is completely bewildered by the revelation that the doctor is actually not his parent. Fatherless and homeless now, Dick leaves the apartment to trudge the streets where his real father had lived:

He started to walk along the street, feeling that he would walk all night, that all the past, all the future was here for him, that he must let the sights, the sounds, the smell of the place seep into him, and maybe as he walked he would feel again that eagerness he had felt coming along the highway when he saw the sweep of the lights and felt as if he had been away for a long time and was coming home.

Callaghan remarks in his prologue to this book, "Many other stories I have written might have been included." Some, like "Big Jules" which appeared in the final edition of *The Best Short Stories* of 1942, are obviously omitted from this 1959 collection because of their similarity to others selected. Many of the stories characteristically deal with love and family relationships. In the words of a distinguished Canadian poet and critic, Margaret Avison, the tales

are the work of an artist with no . . . axe to grind, who makes no . . . concessions to the market's demands. His work *is* popular and powerfully persuasive. The important distinction is that these qualities are by the way, perhaps even unconscious; that a purity of artistic intention is everywhere unmistakable in him. . . .

A single vision encompasses all the people of these stories in all their self-contradictions, betrayals, nobility, bewilderment. It is nothing in the nature of a conclusion—there is unrelieved desolation sometimes, tragedy, absurdity—but every pattern leads out into a larger atmosphere of mercy and wonder. This background is the human context of the Callaghan stories for all their sharp foreground focus. Conveying it is his art.[46]

Morley Callaghan's Stories represents the most substantial collection of his tales to date. It spans nearly thirty years of writing and includes his earliest published work of 1926 as well as one of his latest tales. After 1953 Callaghan virtually stopped writing short stories and turned his full attention to exploring again in depth the themes of justice, guilt and innocence in the novel which eventually became *The Many Colored Coat*.

CHAPTER 8

A Larger Reality

E VEN before the appearance in 1959 of *The Many Colored Coat,* Callaghan was already working on his next novel, *A Passion in Rome*. In 1961 he was shocked by the sudden and tragic death of his former friend, Ernest Hemingway. Although he had not seen or corresponded with Hemingway for some time, memories of their earlier association prompted Callaghan to write *That Summer in Paris*. This biographical reminiscence, already discussed in Chapter Three, was published in 1963. That same year Callaghan began another novel, tentatively entitled *Thumbs Down on Julien Jones,* the background of which is drawn from his intimate knowledge of New York's theatrical world and from his experiences with the Royal Canadian Navy at sea during World War II. Like *A Passion in Rome,* its physical setting extends beyond the North American sphere, and its fictional portrayal of the complexities of modern life promises to be another absorbing presentation of that "larger reality" which transcends the empirical world.

I   *A Passion in Rome* (1961)

In 1958, at the time of Pope Pius XII's death, Callaghan was invited to go to Rome on a journalistic assignment. He stayed for one month, and out of his experiences there shaped the framework for his next and most intricate work of fiction.

A Passion in Rome has been received with violently conflicting opinions from critics: it has been reviewed, on the one hand, as powerful, original, poignant, mature and, on the other hand, as awkward, inept, tedious and obtuse. Such a varied response is perhaps not remarkable for a novel that attempts so much and whose theme embraces life, death and rebirth. Even the title has triple significance. It may be interpreted as representing the passion of Christ being repeated in the agony and death of His Vicar on Earth, as the amorous passion of the two chief characters, and finally as the hero's artistic passion to reshape the heroine's disordered life. The ambiguity of the title is consistent with Callaghan's view of the human condition.

Sam Raymond, frustrated Canadian painter turned newspaper photographer, arrives in Rome to cover the Pope's death. There he becomes intrigued by the idea of trying to rehabilitate a young American of Italian descent who, after her breakdown as a television singer in the United States, has returned to the country of her ancestors. Although Anna Connel (or Carla Caneli, as she calls herself), finding escape from her failure in drink and fantasy, initially distrusts and occasionally rejects Sam's concern, she is eventually restored as a whole woman again through their mutual love. This central passion of the novel is intensified by the setting of the Eternal City at a crucial historical moment when the spiritual heritage and the pageantry of Christianity are sharply contrasted with the pagan glories of the past and the tourist pleasures of the present.

A Passion in Rome reflects a New World infatuation with the ruins, fountains, art, religious spectacle and lively individuality of that metropolis. Rome has obviously cast her spell on Callaghan as on other North American novelists like Hawthorne, James, and Thornton Wilder. Virtually all the underlying images of this story, in which the action is slight compared with the luxuriant metaphorical implication, are directly related to the setting. The city also, perhaps evoking memories of another European city—the Paris of 1929—seems to have embodied for Callaghan the central creative and philosophic concepts which he had evolved during the intervening three decades. In addition to the symbolism suggested by the title, there are at least four other ideas developed at length: the creative power of the artist; man's unquenchable divine spark; the interaction of human lives on one another, and the continuing impact of the past upon the present; and the father-family relationship. These structural images and themes are woven organically into the characterization of the main figures.

Sam Raymond is presented at a critical moment in his life. Thirty-nine years old, after years of hopeful painting, he has realized with a sense of desolation his failure as a creative artist. Driving along the Appian Way from the airport, he is reminded of the elated tones with which an old Canadian painter, Streeter, had advised him a few months earlier to see Michelangelo's work in the Sistine Chapel. This recollection somehow brings a quickening interest to his assignment:

The bus headlights, cutting through the shadows, appeared to be reaching toward the old city now, as he had been reaching for the satisfaction of some gnawing need in himself. And Sam wondered if there couldn't still be some one place in the world where a man's life might take on meaning.[1]

On the day following his first confusing evening in Rome—during which Carla has helped him to obtain a hotel room—Sam hires an interpreter, Francesca Winters, and goes to visit the Sistine Chapel. There, in the ceiling frescoes depicting the Creation, the Fall and the Flood, and in "The Last Judgment" painting covering the wall behind the altar, he finds a deep significance. "Rapt and still as if he half expected the creative force in the finger of God to touch him as it was about to touch the hand of Adam," absorbed in turn by such peripheral figures as the prophets Jonas and Jeremiah and the "Sibyl of Delphi" with her beautiful face, widespread eyes and blue headdress dreaming of the new dispensation of the Christian era, Sam finally stands mute before "the fierce muscular athletic figures, writhing in torment in their faded bluish-greenish ivory colors." [2]

This moving demonstration of creative genius, amusingly punctuated by Francesca's modern tourist chatter, confirms Sam's awareness of his own lack of talent. The experience also arouses a painful realization of all the years during which he had been as much a slave to his artistic hope as was the great Michelangelo:

What did it matter if your own life got distorted as these writhing figures in "The Last Judgment" were distorted? All the loneliness and heartbreak of real life didn't count. Nothing counted but the thing you made. And a man suffering, striving, reaching beyond his grasp, loving and worshiping; if he failed to make the thing that was more important than his miserable life, who cared? Let him go to hell.[3]

It is, however, not this personal bitterness but rather the inspiration and sublimity of Michelangelo which make the deepest impression upon Sam. As he meets again his feminine good Samaritan Carla, he is preoccupied with the association:

All afternoon Michelangelo had been in Sam's mind. And just as before he had imagined the painter dealing with the faces in the Florentine restaurant, he now had him dealing with this girl's face. Right into a corner of "The Last Judgment" she would go, Sam thought, the fingers of demons clutching at her naked body. It made him feel angry. Supposing Michelangelo had been the one wandering in the streets of Rome last night and had met her in the shadow at the corner of a building as he, himself, had done? What would the talent-driven master have made of her? No time for her? Would the great man have taken one glance at her, shaken his head and hurried on? They say he wasn't much interested in women. But the time would come when the giant would search around in his mind for a haunted face and a voluptuous body to put on a damnation fresco; then he would remember the face of the girl on the street. With his tremendous talent he would make her live as long as painting lived. But live as what? God-damn it, live as what? Naturally he would do what he wanted with her. The great talents always did what they wanted with their material. Use it. Something for form and color. A very, very great talent. Who would give a damn about what a girl named Carla Caneli was really like? Supposing she cried out, "That's not me. I don't feel like that"? Who cares? She would die. The work would live on. The work was different, anyway. Again Sam seemed to be caught up in that wild rhythm he had felt in the chapel. He struggled with some strange longing in him he didn't understand himself. Under her mask of discontent and her dreamy vagueness he thought he saw in Carla loneliness and longing. It was the spark of her spirit, he told himself fervently. No painter could ever get it in a glance unless he had some deep feeling for her. Not even Michelangelo. How could the painter bring it out in her if he wasn't able to be there watching it grow in her life? Only a man in love could achieve this masterpiece.[4]

Sam is haunted by the idea that through the power of his love he might recreate a living spirit, not working with pigment but with flesh itself, and thus, like Pygmalion, surpass the achievement of the greatest human artist. Back in his hotel, realizing the full extent of Carla's disintegration, he draws a pencil sketch of her Sibyl-like face illuminated by his vision of her potential radiance. The next day, tormented by this conviction that he could make her life beautiful, he impulsively decides to cancel his flight home and devote himself to reclaiming Carla's life:

"Okay, Angelo," he said to himself grimly. "I came into that chapel of yours expecting a big lift. That finger of God of yours came right down and you stuck it in my eye. Maybe my canvases should all be thrown out. Or some landlady will use them to cover holes in the wall in some cheap rooming house. But maybe it's as big, even a bigger thing to do something with a life—if it moves you—as it is to do something with a hunk of clay or some tubes of paint or some bits of cloth for a uniform. I think I know what Carla should be like." [5]

As the healing influence of Sam's compassionate love restores Carla's self-confidence, he tries jealously to mold her into his own plan without regard for her personal compulsion to test her new confidence by singing in public again. Suddenly he is aware of the sanctity of individual aspiration:

He remembered how he had imagined Michelangelo passing her on the street. And how he himself had longed to do as much for her; no, more for her—something greater than Michelangelo could do on a canvas—transform her so she could have her own being and be free again in her life.[6]

This realization leads Sam to encourage her again in her singing career.

When Carla, eventually reborn as a new woman and no longer in need of his strength, leaves Sam lest his jealous possessiveness toward her destroy him, he finally recognizes with a warm glow of fierce pride that the distorted figures of "The Last Judgment" were "only Michelangelo's best judgment of the matter. Never the last one." [7]

Closely associated with the idea of artistic creativity, as revealed in painting and sculpture, is the motif that man's divine spark is unquenchable. When Sam and Francesca are leaving the Sistine Chapel she remarks:

A long standing place of beauty. Perhaps as good as the race can ever do. But when I think of what one hydrogen bomb dropped around here could also do. . . .

The consolation is . . . that if we're all wiped out the human race returns to God.[8]

Sam grimly rejects this view: "It's not going to be that easy. The great thing is to survive. . . . We just bloody well make the best of it." Later, discussing Carla's past of "humiliation, brutality and despair—all drained through her spirit, all becoming, in spite of herself, summer ripeness," Sam returns to the same topic with Francesca. Out of the ruins of Carla's life "something in her spirit survives. It's got to survive. It's the divine spark. . . . No matter what happens to us, nothing we do or believe can kill off the spark." [9] To the observation of his journalistic colleague that the biggest story is going on at Geneva "where nations are trying to deal with the control of nuclear power . . . with the future of the whole human race" Sam makes a similar comment on the resiliency of the human spirit: "Don't worry, Koster, we'll survive. . . . All I know is there's a spark in us." [10] Even Carla's initial failure in her comeback bid as a singer cannot shake Sam's faith:

Was the spark in her supposed to die in the ruins of a night club; the shambles of one nervous performance under crazily destructive auspices? Did that one ruin mean the unquenchable drive in her for summer ripeness was stilled? No, it couldn't be—it was out of her hands—out of his: it was life itself in them.[11]

On this mysterious and eternal spirit of man, with its incalculable potential for the future, all the forces of the past are working. In modern Rome the myths of Alba Longa are still alive. The Italian people to Sam seem to reflect vividly their history. Carla's beautifully irregular face strikingly resembles Michelangelo's "Sibyl of Delphi" whose design Sam, in foreshadowing fascination, had traced out with his hands in the Sistine Chapel. Carla's lineaments suggest "the patrician and peasant bloodlines crossed. Something done in a quick passion in a dark alley a thousand years ago." [12] In her fantasy she becomes with Sam a legendary Roman woman and seeks refuge in the city's early grandeur: "Among the ruins, telling him lively and intimate stories about dead old Romans, she could have him with her, yet forget her abject need of him. . . . The place where they seemed best able to meet each other was in the timeless past." [13] As the victim of modern promoters she is symbolically like the mythical Tarpeia: "Tarpeia goes all out for the Sabines, and who is it pushed her off the rock? The Sabines, of course." [14] Carla's own unhappy story—told, significantly, as she stands in the darkness of the Capitoline Hill looking down on the city "as if it held the world of her childhood" [15]—is also the history of Rome: rape, sack and resurrection.

One of the most vividly developed individual images linking the past to the present is used when Carla introduces Sam to the Coliseum by night:

In the floodlights the great wall shone in a ghostly silver light, tapering off, jagged-edged, into the darkness; and above was the blanket of the Roman night. . . .

After the floodlights on the outside it was like entering a pitch-black cave. Standing beside her, he waited for his eyes to get used to the light, and heard the rustling of her paper bag as she opened it. At first he could only see the rim and the highest row of stone seats in the starlight, then gradually as it got lighter, he could make out the descending tiers. In the shadows they were like the pock-marked face of the moon. Before him stretched the blackness of the field itself. In the ghostly gray and black stillness there was no sound now, not even the rustling of the bag. She tossed out a piece of meat. Nothing moved; not a sound. Then in the darkness he saw glowing eyes. He felt a little chill on his neck. As she kept tossing out the pieces of meat, eyes shone in the darkness to the left and right of him. A cat snarled, and he jumped. The fierce spitting scratching anger of hungry cats fighting for meat made him shiver. . . .

The flashing eyes in the shadows, the snarling, then the glint of moonlight on the tiers of seats, made him draw back, and his mind played tricks on him. The whole arena seemed to come alive; it seemed to be there in a reddish glow as the fierce sun was strained through the giant colored awnings of the poles around the arena; and the wild animals, the leopards, the wolves, the cheetahs and the tigers were there, circling around crazily, blind with fright, sliding frantically along the barricade, crashing into it, lashing out with their tails; and now waiting with wild glowing eyes, watching him because he was standing over the underground cells where the prisoners, doomed to be tossed out as meat, waited. The fear and the terrible anxiety of the prisoners was like a smell seeping through the ground to him, and there before him, waiting with glowing eyes, half-starved, the great cats.[16]

This arresting scene, and the hallucination which it inspires in
Sam's mind, strikes a note which recurs often in Callaghan's writings. Like the zoo in *It's Never Over,* the Coliseum is a reminder of
man's primordial heritage of violence which reaches back to the
jungle itself.

The occasion of the Pope's death intensifies this montage of past
and present. The cortege is "like watching a story book opening
up . . . like all that has happened here in Rome in the last fifteen
hundred years; it's like having it all in a parade from long ago and
having it all come slowly toward you." [17] After its ruined glory, a
dead Rome "was born again under the popes." The only capital of
the ancient empires to regain its stature as a world center, it is to
Sam "the city that conquered time." [18] The surge of the crowd towards St. Peter's is "the Roman mob just as it was two thousand
years ago. . . . This is the place where Caligula's chariots used to
race, and somewhere over there by the church had been Nero's
Circus; it had always been a place of screams and passions and
death." [19] When the police let some hundreds through the barricade, Sam is almost hypnotized by their charge:

Maybe it was the dusk, the lowering sky, the great shadows from the
church falling over the square, the huge slabs of stone rising beside
him while his ears were filled with the sound of pounding feet. Then
the light from the open door reached to the broken line of faces coming
closer, almost upon him, and in a moment of strange panic, he froze—
breathless—waiting to be engulfed, utterly alone and alien; and in him
a frantic protest that he was alone.[20]

Epitomized in this incident is the predicament of man as a creature who cannot escape the influence of his ancestors or of his
own contemporaries, even though as an individual he must stand
alone.

In the final drama of the funeral, when with a strange incongruity the hammering of the workmen noisily sealing the coffin
drowns out the eulogy, Sam sees in his imagination "the shadowy
figures of others in antique processions, precursors of those he saw
now, who were perhaps saying as the others had said, that man
was a unique creature on earth because he was aware of the mystery of existence and death." [21] As the coffin sinks slowly into the

crypt, the hammering of the workmen, the burial rites repeated by the priests and the rapt attention of the spectators all seem to become intelligible to Sam: "Even in the ruins of death they were hurling the challenge to eternity, 'We *still* live.'" [22]

The father-family and especially the father-child relationship is another image which runs throughout *A Passion in Rome*. The impending death of the Pope, the Vicar of Christ, will make the Church a widow. "But a widow who'll have a new bridegroom." [23] The new Pope's election brings happiness to the Roman people "like the joy of children and women of a house, eager for the love of a new master." [24] "Rome's papa," the Holy Father, is dying just as Sam's own father, famous painter of the "Date with Destiny" portraits, is ailing. Carla's story of Hadrian's fondness for the boy whom he considered almost a son, "the one who was drowned in Egypt. . . . swimming out and away from him," [25] is ironically reminiscent of Sam's estrangement from his own father. The nomadic fathers of Carla's childhood find a parallel in the changing temporal and religious heads of Rome. In the life of both city and individual the place of paternal love is significant. The Pope assumes for Carla the role of a father; and her progress from fantasy and despair to hopeful self-dependence has a relationship to his changing condition. Her disastrous singing debut coincides with his death. On this same night, in which she dies to her former self, she no longer needs that "certitude she sought in her sexual appeal." [26] Her confident assurance of spiritual restoration, manifested in the decision to leave Sam, occurs simultaneously with the election of the new Pope.

Scattered everywhere throughout the novel are individual images that reinforce these basic symbols or foreshadow the action. On Sam's first night in Rome, after his initial encounter with Carla, he sees her outside the hotel with Alberto: "The angry man was scolding her. Then he gripped her arm, trying to lead her away into the shadows, and she jerked her arm free. Half turning she looked back at the lighted doorway where Sam stood." [27] This little episode is a preview of the future in the same way that Sam's pencil sketch of Carla points to her final transformation: "The face on the sheet gradually took on an expression of secret, mysterious, almost arrogantly untroubled self-possession." [28] Just as symbolical is Sam's meeting with the ailing Alberto at the square at Trastevere to negotiate over Carla. The entire scene presents a series of contrasts: the restaurant, the smells of garbage and the church of Santa Maria where a funeral party waits to enter while a wedding party leaves. Later, in another restaurant in Trastevere, the shavings which Sam took for luck from the stove in the Sistine Chapel become a favorable omen of Carla's rehabilitation as a singer. Playfully putting them on a plate and lighting them, she remarks significantly, "The chips are down." [29] Minutes after Sam has pronounced the smoke to be white—the signal of happy agreement—she performs with ease and confidence again to an appreciative audience.

A final example of this plethora of imagistic pictures is presented in Sam's last hours in Rome. Walking once more through the same streets he had roamed with Carla, he realizes why she has decided to leave him. He finds in the sight of the bright-eyed, wrinkled old woman "squatted on the ground beside her charcoal brazier on which she cooked chestnuts" a pictorial vignette of continuing life. Framed behind by the ruins of the past, her old eyes are full of life and in the bright flames which she stirred Carla's face seems to appear. [30]

Callaghan's employment of color in this book is unusual and striking. In addition to the customary interplay of light and darkness there is also a profusion of Mediterranean hues. The pink, sun-drenched yellow and lime-greens of gay *Italia* contrast with the bold red, blue and gold of Renaissance art as well as with the deep purple of ecclesiastical robes and the brilliantly multi-colored uniforms worn at the Pope's funeral. This attention to color is part of the over-all richness of description and symbol which pervades the book and leaves the critical reader almost over-powered. In the words of an English reviewer, "It's far too glam-ourous." [31]

Despite this glamour, much of which stems from Callaghan's haunting evocation of Rome, the story is realistic and authentic. Although its organization on so many levels of allegorical and overt meaning makes it almost a *tour de force,* the novel is full of the comic incongruity of life itself. Misjudgments, the irony of human vanity and pettiness, earthly concerns and spiritual aspirations all form a plausible part of the characters' lives. Satirical thrusts on a wide variety of targets—national traits (the comically mercenary streak of Italians and the indistinguishable identity of Canadians abroad), American tourists with their vulgar air of opulence, the pretended piety of the indifferent, pickpockets everywhere in the crowds of the devout, and the bumbling hierarchy (even the inept embalming of the Pope and the confusion of the Conclave's smoke signals do not escape), stereotyped academic training or journalistic research—emerge naturally in dialogue that catches the rhythm of current idiom. "The author's insight into his characters is always present in the things they say, or say to each other. . . . the poise is held." [32]

Not all critics, however, have interpreted *A Passion in Rome* as favorably as this. Typical of the consideration which Callaghan's work has sometimes received is the review in *The New York Times Book Review*, written by Robert Gorham Davis, teacher and critic of modern fiction at Columbia University. It is worth quoting at some length the comments of Professor Davis:

Great events and strong feelings do not by themselves produce great novels. There have to be characters, and the characters have to have consciousness, and the consciousness has to be expressed in words. For a subject such as Mr. Callaghan attempts, this consciousness should be informed and discriminating. The characters' capacity of being finely aware, Henry James said, as Lear and Hamlet were finely aware, "makes absolutely the intensity of their adventure, gives the maximum of sense to what befalls them". . . . The characters here, however, are anything but finely aware. Totally inadequate to the demands made upon them, they are insensitive, vulgar, and above all unconvincing. . . .

When Sam sees the Sistine Chapel, he wonders what Michelangelo would have thought of Carla, and decides to devote his own artistic energies to making something of her, to restoring her confidence. He thinks all will be solved if she can sing in intimate night clubs and the better class of restaurant. Rather Walter Mittyish scenes follow in which Sam tells off the Italian movie producer, an American gangster, a powerful New York agent and assorted minor characters. He is strong on tough talk: "Tell her I'll come back here and kick her teeth out!" Carla's language is even earthier.

Some of the mass scenes are well done, and there are a few affecting passages between Carla and Sam. Very disturbing, however, is the involvement of the dead Pope's image with Sam's erotic designs on Carla. "A Passion in Rome" most effectively teaches that the more ambitious the author's theme and subject, the more masterly must be his observation, reflection, art, learning and taste. If he cannot summon up such powers, then far better a good minor novel than a bad "major" one.[33]

In this article Mr. Davis has touched upon certain aspects of Callaghan's fiction which have concerned other reviewers of his novels. They have often concentrated on his minor faults and failed to appreciate the amplitude of his design. Critics have looked for the characters or narrative to be developed along their own lines, and have sometimes drawn conclusions which cannot be substantiated by the text. The careful reader, for example, searches in vain for any passage in which Sam "tells off the Italian movie producer." Actually, Sam carefully avoids arousing Alberto's animus in order not to jeopardize his cooperation in releasing Carla. The statement, "the involvement of the dead Pope's image with Sam's erotic designs on Carla" is "very disturbing," is likely to strike a reader as either surprising or absurd.

In *A Passion in Rome* Callaghan is experimenting with a novel that is different from any which he had previously attempted. Its symbolism is boldly exposed because he is deliberately treading the fine line between realistic fiction and allegory. In some ways the book may be considered as an allegorical history and interpretation of human conscience. It is also an absorbing and poignant human drama, a searching appreciation of the mystery and power of the Christian tradition, and almost a compendium of the author's opinions about life. Many of the ideas which find expression in this novel had already been introduced or explored in earlier works: the sanctity of the individual; self-awareness,[34] personal perception and the right to self-expression;[35] the need to love and be loved; the dismissal of the myth of innocence[36] and of the "old lie that life was a sorrowful business, that all desire led to sorrow";[37] the view that all the past has significance for the present; and the belief that the only security is to possess one's own soul in peace. Even Sam's advice to Carla, "You have to protect your own talent with a little arrogance. To hell with trying to please people," [38] is a reflection of Callaghan's own artistic conviction. These perennial topics of mutual and ultimate concern are constantly being tested in the experience of his characters. Like

Dr. Johnson, Callaghan in an age of rapidly shifting values strives never to lose sight of fundamentals. In *A Passion in Rome*, without foregoing his humanity or becoming doctrinaire, he has assessed the present in terms of the past and in the process cleared his readers' minds of a great deal of cant. In his conclusion he has also left them with "the eternally unquenchable promise of spring. The real magic on earth." [39]

II *The Way It Is: Callaghan's Literary Image*

Ever since Boswell, whose biography made the figure of Dr. Johnson striding through the streets of London or dominating the conversation of the drawing room as familiar as his published work, the reputation of an author has been closely associated with his personal life. This trend has been accentuated in twentieth-century America by the impact of modern media of communication. The private lives of writers, like those of movie actors, are matters of constant curiosity. Callaghan's older literary contemporaries became international celebrities. Scott and Zelda Fitzgerald's extravagantly exotic life with its disintegration into alcoholism and schizophrenia was almost as symbolic of the Jazz Age to the American public as *The Great Gatsby* itself. The elegiac world of war, bull-fighting and big-game hunting of Hemingway's writings became inextricably woven with the myth that surrounded his own life.

The history of Callaghan's image is charged with irony. His literary reputation was jeopardized from the very beginning when *Scribner's Magazine* in its enthusiastic introduction of this "New Fiction Star" linked him with Hemingway. The effects of this gratuitous association are not yet obliterated. Almost every review of Callaghan's early works, and even of many of his later writings, contains the inevitable, and too often irrelevant, mention of Hemingway. Many critics, indeed, in their confidence of the similarity of style in these two writers never bothered to examine carefully Callaghan's work. Their reviews are full of inaccuracies and misinterpretations because they failed to see that his fictional technique is highly original. Recently Callaghan has taken the opportunity, presented by *That Summer in Paris* and his review of Hemingway's *A Moveable Feast*, to clarify "The Way It Was." Callaghan's article, entitled "An Ocean Away," which appeared in the *Times Literary Supplement* issue of June 4, 1964, has thrown further light on the important literary influences of his early years as a writer.

In 1965 it is possible to survey some forty years of Callaghan's writings with a measure of historical perspective and to assess "the way it is." From the current vantage point his career seems to have a definable pattern: a brilliant beginning in the twenties and a sustained output until just before World War II; a fallow decade until nearly the end of the forties; and a still unfinished outburst of creativity in the fifties and sixties. In addition to more than a hundred short stories in leading North American and European magazines he has published sixteen books: nine full-length novels, a juvenile novel, a fictionalized account of the University of Toronto, a privately printed novella, a biographical reminiscence and three collections of short stories.

Despite this considerable body of work Callaghan's reputation has undergone vicissitude. He began as a literary prodigy, acclaimed as a master of the short story and frequently compared with Tolstoy and Chekhov. Even to the present day no critic of distinction has seriously challenged this judgment. Perhaps Wyndham Lewis' tribute of the mid-thirties, which was published in *Saturday Night* and partially reprinted on the dust jacket of *Morley Callaghan's Stories* (1959), best sums up the accepted critical view of this aspect of his writing:

These are tales very full of human sympathy—a blending of all the events of life into a pattern of tolerance and of mercy; there is no sultry misanthropic phobia lurking anywhere in it. . . .

Apart from the literary merit of the stories, this book [*Now That April's Here*] is beautifully replete with a message of human tolerance and love. Every one, or almost all, of these discrete miniature dramas ends softly and gently. At the end of some anguish there is peace; at the end of some bitter dispute there is reconciliation. All of these creatures are dimly aware that the parts they play—for all the sound and fury into which they may be led by the malice of nature, by the demands of the instinct for animal survival, or by our terrible heritage of original sin—the roles they are called upon to take are played according to some great law, within the bounds of a rational order. The plot, however tragic, is not some diabolic and meaningless phantasy, in other words—which is the fatal conclusion that we are required to draw from the perusal of a story, say of Mr. Hemingway's. There is good and evil not merely good luck and bad luck. And if they end in a witty sally or in a comic deflation, the wit and the comic deflation are full of a robust benevolence.

Although his short stories have been widely applauded and have appeared in anthologies around the world, the verdict on the novels has not been unanimously approving. In the *Canadian Annual Review of 1960* Professor Milton Wilson succinctly sums up Callaghan's reputation in his own country to that date:

When the internationals liked him, the locals didn't; when his voice and face became familiar on radio and television, his books wouldn't sell; when the Canadian public was apathetic, the academics wrote about him and put him on courses; when all men decided to praise him, the Montreal reviewers still cried woe—because a Torontonian had the temerity to write about Montreal.

These hostile Montreal reviewers, like many readers, were undoubtedly disappointed with Callaghan's novels because they often present unusual and unexpected aspects of familiar settings or concepts. A style deceptively simple on the surface, and frequently criticized as monotonous or journalistic, seems to invite the reader to anticipate a conventionally happy ending. Cheated of this satisfaction, a superficial reader may feel that he, as well as the hero or heroine, has been left in a vacuum by the dénouements of Callaghan's novels. Yet his fictional resolutions, if they are interpreted in terms of the concept that individual self-fulfillment and growth in self-awareness are more important than the accidental events of life or even than death itself, are logical and inevitable.

In *That Summer in Paris* Callaghan discusses his view of "the right relationship between the words and the thing or person being described: the words should be as transparent as glass, and every time a writer used a brilliant phrase to prove himself witty or clever he merely took the mind of the reader away from the object and directed it to himself." Comparing Callaghan with his older literary associates, Edmund Wilson in his review of *That Summer in Paris* in *The New Yorker* makes this same point:

His powers of observation, so quiet but so alert, were never blinded by the dazzling performances that these two great actors of the twenties spent so much of their time putting on. Fitzgerald and Hemingway were both romantics; they lived in semi-adolescent fantasies. Each of them was rather a poet who put himself at the center of his poem than, as Morley Callaghan was, a sober inquirer into what went on in other people's minds; but in Callaghan's less brilliantly imagined world, as we know from his excellent novels, the man himself is not at the center as a self-assertive, self-conscious ego which must force the world to come to terms with it and, whether in success or failure, to recognize its incomparable importance. Who *is* the writer Morley Callaghan, the reader of his books might well ask, as he could not possibly ask of Hemingway or of Fitzgerald. Callaghan is so much interested in moral character as exhibited in other people's behavior that, unlike his two exhibitionistic friends, he never shows himself at all. The people in his stories do not burst upon us as they do in Scott Fitzgerald or incise themselves as they do in Hemingway; gently but very surely they lay hold on the reader's attention and gradually become more interesting, become something often startlingly different from what we had at first supposed, and the situations seem to unfold almost without the author's manipulation. Callaghan has nothing of the lyricism that intoxicated the readers of his two older colleagues, and the rhythms of his prose, though they carry one, do not generate the same kind of emotion, but his unobtrusive art is more subtle and his intelligence more mature than those of either of the others.

Other contemporary American critics like Alfred Kazin and writers like Erskine Caldwell and James T. Farrell have added their praise to swell Callaghan's growing reputation as a novelist. Some of his books have been reprinted in England and have appeared in translation in various European countries, where they have been received with enthusiasm.

In Canada, too, Callaghan's compatriots are paying a belated tribute to their most distinguished novelist. In 1960 Callaghan was awarded the Lorne Pierce Medal for Literature by the Royal Society of Canada. The citation given to him on that occasion and written by Frank R. Scott, himself a distinguished poet and critic, is a fitting commentary on Callaghan's career:

With the appearance of Morley Callaghan's first novel *Strange Fugitive* in 1928, Canadian fiction could no longer be regarded as a pale extension of the English tradition. For with this book—and the short stories and novels that followed in the thirties—Callaghan broke open for us the egg-shell of our cultural colonialism. He went to Paris (instead of London), consorted with the international literary set and came home by way of New York. However, he *did* come home, and his fiction, for all of its sophistication of vision and technique, is instinct with place—our place—and with time—our time. . . .

Morley Callaghan is one of the very few Canadian writers to have earned a solid and sure international reputation and his work has been translated into several languages.

Never pretentious, indeed deceptively simple in structure and tone, Mr. Callaghan's fiction is informed by a deep sense of pathos and the dignity of the human condition, and controlled by a vision of life which might be called one of "compassionate irony." Here, surely, is an individual voice. Here, already, is a body of work which will endure.

Since the Royal Society of Canada's salute, Callaghan has published two more novels and an autobiographical reminiscence. At sixty-two his physical and imaginative vitality give promise of continuing with undiminished vigor. However critics and posterity evaluate his future work or assess his total career, his place as a world author is beyond dispute.

Notes and References

Chapter One

1. Robert Weaver, "A Talk with Morley Callaghan," *The Tamarack Review*, 7 (Spring 1958), pp. 3-29, includes interesting details of this early period.
2. *That Summer in Paris* (New York: Coward-McCann Incorporated, 1963), pp. 13-14.
3. *Ibid.*, p. 19.
4. At one time Hemingway proposed to base a satiric novel on Hindmarsh, to be entitled *The Son-in-Law*.
5. *That Summer in Paris*, p. 29.
6. *Ibid.*, pp. 60-61.
7. *Strange Fugitive* (New York: Charles Scribner's Sons, 1928), p. 102.
8. *Ibid.*, p. 11.
9. *Ibid.*, pp. 73-74.
10. *Ibid.*, pp. 72-73.
11. *Ibid.*, p. 141.
12. *Ibid.*, pp. 78-79.
13. *Ibid.*, p. 94.
14. *Ibid.*, p. 204.
15. *That Summer in Paris*, pp. 19-20.
16. *Strange Fugitive*, p. 160.
17. *Ibid.*

Chapter Two

1. Robert Weaver, "A Talk with Morley Callaghan," *The Tamarack Review*, 7 (Spring 1958), p. 17.
2. *Ibid.*, p. 21.
3. *Ibid.*, p. 23.
4. In the ending of "A Cocky Young Man."
5. John Chamberlain, "Morley Callaghan's Inarticulate People," *New York Times Book Review*, Mar. 24, 1929, p. 9.

6. Sean O'Faolain, *The Short Story* (London: Collins, 1948), p. 38.

7. Robert Weaver, "A Talk with Morley Callaghan," *The Tamarack Review*, 7 (Spring 1958), p. 17.

8. *Ibid.*

9. *Scribner's Magazine*, LXXXIV, No. 1 (July 1928), p. 37.

10. June Callwood, "The Many Coloured Career of Morley Callaghan," *Star Weekly*, Dec. 17, 1960, p. 17.

11. Charles A. Fenton, *The Apprenticeship of Ernest Hemingway* (New York: Farrar, Straus and Young, 1954), p. 93.

12. *A Native Argosy* (New York: Charles Scribner's Sons, 1929), p. 346.

Chapter Three

1. *That Summer in Paris*, p. 69.

2. *Ibid.*, pp. 94-95.

3. *Ibid.*, p. 95.

4. *Ibid.*, pp. 125-26.

5. *Ibid.*, p. 147.

6. *Ibid.*, p. 148.

7. *It's Never Over* (New York: Charles Scribner's Sons, 1930), p. 47.

8. *Ibid.*, p. 42.

9. *Ibid.*, p. 90.

10. *Ibid.*, p. 186.

11. *Ibid.*, p. 188.

12. *Ibid.*, p. 221.

13. *Ibid.*, p. 141.

Chapter Four

1. *A Broken Journey* (New York: Charles Scribner's Sons, 1932), p. 22.

2. *Ibid.*, p. 2.

3. *Ibid.*, p. 3.

4. *Ibid.*, p. 225.

5. *Ibid.*, p. 255.

6. *Ibid.*, pp. 109-10.

7. *Ibid.*, pp. 53-54.

8. *Ibid.*, p. 202.

9. *Ibid.*, pp. 223-24.

10. *Ibid.*, p. 14.

11. *Ibid.*, p. 109.

12. *Ibid.*, p. 145.

13. *Ibid.*, p. 227.

14. *Ibid.*, p. 23.

15. *Ibid.*, pp. 40-41.

16. *Ibid.*, p. 99.

17. *Ibid.*, pp. 207-08.

18. *Editor to Author. The Letters of Maxwell E. Perkins* (New York: Charles Scribner's Sons, 1950), pp. 74-77.

19. *That Summer in Paris*, p. 20.

20. *Such Is My Beloved* (New York: Charles Scribner's Sons, 1934), pp. 1-2.

21. *Ibid.*, p. 27.

22. *Ibid.*, p. 195.

23. *Ibid.*, p. 262.

24. *Ibid.*, p. 58.

25. *Ibid.*, p. 35.

26. *Ibid.*, pp. 139-40.

27. *Ibid.*, p. 190.

28. *Ibid.*, p. 188.

29. *Ibid.*, pp. 253-54.

30. *Ibid.*, p. 244.

31. *Ibid.*, p. 91.

32. *Ibid.*, p. 261.

33. *Ibid.*, p. 237.

34. *They Shall Inherit The Earth* (New York: The Macmillan Company, 1935), p. 127.

35. *Ibid.*, p. 30.

36. *Ibid.*, p. 36.

37. *Ibid.*, pp. 212-13.

38. *Ibid.*, p. 309.

39. *Ibid.*, p. 320.

40. *Ibid.*, p. 194.

41. *Ibid.*, p. 134.

42. *Ibid.*, p. 135.

43. *Ibid.*, p. 227.

44. *Ibid.*, p. 246.

45. *Ibid.*, p. 105.

46. *Ibid.*, p. 248.

47. *Ibid.*, p. 253.

48. *Ibid.*, p. 256.

49. *Ibid.*, p. 258.

50. *Ibid.*, p. 259.

51. *Ibid.*, p. 113.

52. *Ibid.*, p. 310.

53. *Ibid.*, p. 326.

54. *Ibid.*, p. 216.

55. *Ibid.*, p. 16.

56. *Ibid.*, p. 117; see also p. 121.

57. *Ibid.*, p. 311.

58. *Ibid.*, p. 203.

59. *Ibid.*, p. 309.

60. *Ibid.*, p. 250; see also p. 114.

61. *Ibid.*, p. 24.

62. *Ibid.*, p. 179.

63. *Ibid.*, pp. 285-86.

64. *Ibid.*, p. 20.

65. *Ibid.*, p. 152.

66. Robert Weaver, "A Talk with Morley Callaghan," *The Tamarack Review*, 7 (Spring 1958), p. 23.

Chapter Five

1. *That Summer in Paris*, p. 132. Four of the stories from *Now That April's Here* ("A Sick Call," "The Rejected One," "Rocking Chair" and "Silk Stockings") were made into a movie by a Toronto firm. With Raymond Massey as narrator, this film was shown in various Canadian cities during the late forties.

2. See above, pp. 75-76.

3. Robert Weaver, "A Talk with Morley Callaghan," *The Tamarack Review*, 7 (Spring 1958), p. 24.

4. *More Joy in Heaven* (New York: Random House, 1937), pp. 275-76. A television version of this novel was presented serially in six half-hour installments by the Canadian Broadcasting Corporation during the spring of 1964.

5. *Ibid.*, p. 247.

6. *Ibid.*, p. 154.

7. *Ibid.*, p. 53.

8. *Ibid.*, p. 93.

9. *Ibid.*, p. 111.

10. *Ibid.*, p. 119.

11. *Ibid.*, p. 225.

12. *Ibid.*, p. 270.

13. *Ibid.*, p. 273.

14. *Ibid.*, p. 277.

15. *Ibid.*, p. 207.

16. *Ibid.*, p. 97.

17. *Ibid.*, p. 271.

18. *Ibid.*, p. 36.

19. *Ibid.*, p. 210.

20. *Ibid.*, p. 238.
21. *Ibid.*, pp. 19-20.
22. *Ibid.*, p. 132.
23. *Ibid.*, p. 155.
24. *Ibid.*, pp. 276-77.
25. *Ibid.*, p. 177.

Chapter Six

1. Robert Weaver, "A Talk with Morley Callaghan," *The Tamarack Review*, 7 (Spring 1958), p. 20. See also Callaghan's own comments on his career during these fallow years in "The Pleasures of Failure," *Maclean's Magazine*, 78 (March 6, 1965), pp. 12 ff.
2. "Ends and Means and Aldous Huxley," *The Canadian Forum*, 17 (March 1938), pp. 422-23.
3. "Little Marxist, What Now?" *Saturday Night*, 54 (Sept. 16, 1939), p. 24.
4. "Thomas Wolfe's Appetite for Life," *Saturday Night*, 54 (July 15, 1939), p. 8.
5. "If Civilization Must Be Saved," *Saturday Night*, 55 (Dec. 16, 1939), p. 6.
6. June Callwood, "The Many Coloured Career of Morley Callaghan," *Star Weekly*, Dec. 17, 1960, p. 17.
7. *Luke Baldwin's Vow* (Philadelphia: The John C. Winston Company, 1948), p. 110.
8. *Ibid.*, p. 187.
9. *The Varsity Story* (Toronto: The Macmillan Company of Canada, 1948), pp. 114-15.

Chapter Seven

1. Hugo McPherson, "The Two Worlds of Morley Callaghan: Man's Earthly Quest," *Queen's Quarterly*, 64 (Autumn 1957), p. 352.
2. *The Loved and The Lost* (New York: The Macmillan Company, 1951), p. 1.
3. *Ibid.*, p. 131.
4. *Ibid.*, p. 135.
5. *Ibid.*, p. 32.
6. *Ibid.*, pp. 69-70.
7. *Ibid.*, pp. 165-66.
8. *Ibid.*, p. 153.
9. *Ibid.*, p. 232.
10. *Ibid.*, p. 228.
11. *Ibid.*, p. 164.

12. *The Many Colored Coat* (New York: Coward-McCann Incorporated, 1960), pp. 154, 206 and 255.

13. Edmund Wilson, "Morley Callaghan of Toronto," *The New Yorker*, XXXVI, 41 (November 26, 1960), p. 232.

14. *The Many Colored Coat*, p. 182.

15. *Ibid.*, pp. 175 and 193.

16. *Ibid.*, pp. 119 and 217.

17. *Ibid.*, pp. 120 and 192.

18. *Ibid.*, pp. 160 and 218.

19. *Ibid.*, pp. 160 and 213.

20. *Ibid.*, pp. 190 and 248.

21. *Ibid.*, p. 18.

22. *Ibid.*, p. 106.

23. *Ibid.*, p. 138.

24. *Ibid.*, p. 129.

25. *Ibid.*, p. 226.

26. *Ibid.*, pp. 24-25.

27. *Ibid.*, p. 20.

28. *Ibid.*, p. 35.

29. *Ibid.*, p. 99.

30. *Ibid.*, p. 172.

31. *Ibid.*, p. 257.

32. *Ibid.*, p. 313.

33. *Ibid.*, p. 86.

34. *Ibid.*, p. 316.

35. *Ibid.*, p. 259.

36. *Ibid.*, p. 85.

37. *Ibid.*, p. 230.

38. *Ibid.*, p. 107.

39. *Ibid.*, p. 174.

40. *Ibid.*, p. 186.

41. *Ibid.*, p. 314.

42. *Ibid.*, pp. 280-81.

43. *Ibid.*, p. 314.

44. *Ibid.*, p. 261.

45. *Ibid.*, p. 100.

46. Margaret Avison, "Callaghan Revisited," *The Canadian Forum*, 39 (March 1960), pp. 276-77.

Chapter Eight

1. *A Passion in Rome* (New York: Coward-McCann Incorporated, 1961), p. 10.

2. *Ibid.*, pp. 36-37.

3. *Ibid.*, pp. 38-39.
4. *Ibid.*, pp. 54-55.
5. *Ibid.*, p. 65.
6. *Ibid.*, p. 183.
7. *Ibid.*, p. 352.
8. *Ibid.*, p. 40.
9. *Ibid.*, p. 196.
10. *Ibid.*, p. 205.
11. *Ibid.*, p. 258.
12. *Ibid.*, p. 70.
13. *Ibid.*, p. 133.
14. *Ibid.*, p. 170.
15. *Ibid.*, p. 173.
16. *Ibid.*, pp. 153-55.
17. *Ibid.*, p. 252.
18. *Ibid.*, p. 231.
19. *Ibid.*, p. 266.
20. *Ibid.*, p. 269.
21. *Ibid.*, pp. 286-87.
22. *Ibid.*, p. 288.
23. *Ibid.*, p. 242.
24. *Ibid.*, p. 333.
25. *Ibid.*, p. 135.
26. *Ibid.*, p. 120.
27. *Ibid.*, p. 22.
28. *Ibid.*, p. 61.
29. *Ibid.*, p. 302.
30. *Ibid.*, p. 346.
31. Anthony Ward, "A Way of Feeling," *The Spectator,* 7083 (March 27, 1964), p. 422.
32. *Ibid.*
33. Robert Gorham Davis, "Carla, Sam and a Dying Pope," *The New York Times Book Review* (October 15, 1961), pp. 4 and 30.
34. *A Passion in Rome,* p. 172.
35. *Ibid.*, p. 165.
36. *Ibid.*, p. 194.
37. *Ibid.*, p. 46.
38. *Ibid.*, p. 178.
39. *Ibid.*, p. 195.

Selected Bibliography

PRIMARY SOURCES

1. Books by Morley Callaghan, Chronologically Arranged

Strange Fugitive. New York: Scribners, and Grosset and Dunlap, 1928.

A Native Argosy. New York: Scribners, and Toronto: Macmillan, 1929.

It's Never Over. New York: Scribners, and Toronto: Macmillan, 1930.

No Man's Meat. Paris: Black Manikin Press, 1931. Autographed limited edition.

A Broken Journey. New York: Scribners, and Toronto: Macmillan, 1932.

Such Is My Beloved. New York: Scribners, and Toronto: Macmillan, 1934. Reprinted in "New Canadian Library" series, with Introduction by Malcolm Ross, by McClelland and Stewart of Toronto, 1957.

They Shall Inherit The Earth. New York and Toronto: Macmillan, 1935. Reprinted in "Modern Age Books," 1937, and in "New Canadian Library" series, with Introduction by Frank W. Watt, by McClelland and Stewart of Toronto, 1962.

Now That April's Here and Other Stories. New York: Random House, and Toronto: Macmillan, 1936.

More Joy in Heaven. New York: Random House, and Toronto: Macmillan, 1937. Reprinted in "New Canadian Library" series, with Introduction by Hugo McPherson, by McClelland and Stewart of Toronto, 1960.

Luke Baldwin's Vow. Philadelphia and Toronto: Winston, 1948.

The Varsity Story. Toronto: Macmillan, 1948.

The Loved and The Lost. New York and Toronto: Macmillan, 1951. Reprinted as a Signet Book in "The New American Library," 1952. London: MacGibbon and Kee, 1961.

"The Man With The Coat." *Maclean's Magazine,* LXVIII, 8 (April 16, 1955).

Morley Callaghan's Stories. Toronto: Macmillan, 1959. London: Mac-
Gibbon and Kee, 2 vols., 1962.

The Many Colored Coat. New York: Coward-McCann, and Toronto:
Macmillan, 1960. London: MacGibbon and Kee, 1963.

A Passion in Rome. New York: Coward-McCann, and Toronto: Macmillan, 1961. Reprinted by Dell of New York, 1962. London: Mac-
Gibbon and Kee, 1964.

That Summer in Paris. New York: Coward-McCann, and Toronto:
Macmillan, 1963. London: MacGibbon and Kee, 1964. Reprinted
by Dell of New York, 1964.

2. Plays

"Turn Again Home" (produced in 1950 in Toronto under the title "Going Home"). Unpublished typed manuscript. Written 1939.

"Just Ask for George" (produced in 1949 in Toronto under the title
"To Tell the Truth"). Unpublished typed manuscript. Written
1939.

3. Selected Articles

"An Ocean Away." *Times Literary Supplement,* No. 3, 249 (June 4,
1964), 493. An account of authors who influenced Callaghan's
style.

"Ends and Means and Aldous Huxley." *The Canadian Forum,* 17
(March 1938), 422-23.

"If Civilization Must Be Saved." *Saturday Night,* 55 (December 16,
1938), 6.

"Little Marxist, What Now?" *Saturday Night,* 54 (September 16,
1939), 24.

"Novelist." *Writing in Canada.* Toronto: Macmillan, 1956.

"The Ontario Story: Paradox of Progress." *Saturday Night,* 70 (November 12, 1955), 7-8. Includes memories of youthful experiences
in various parts of the province.

"The Pleasures of Failure." *Maclean's Magazine,* 78 (March 6, 1965),
12 ff.

"The Plight of Canadian Fiction." *The University of Toronto Quarterly,* 7 (January 1938), 152-61.

"The Way It Was." *The Spectator,* No. 7071 (May 22, 1964), 696. A
review of Hemingway's *A Moveable Feast* with comments on the
early career of that writer.

"Thomas Wolfe's Appetite for Life." *Saturday Night,* 54 (July 15,
1939), 8.

Selected Bibliography

SECONDARY SOURCES

Selected Books and Articles

Avison, Margaret. "Callaghan Revisited." *The Canadian Forum,* 39 (March 1960), 276-77.

Callwood, June. "The Many Coloured Career of Morley Callaghan." Toronto *Star Weekly,* December 17, 1960, 16-19.

Chamberlain, John. "Morley Callaghan's Inarticulate People." *The New York Times Book Review,* March 24, 1929, 9.

Cheyer, A. H. "Morley Callaghan." *Wilson Library Bulletin,* 36 (November 1961), 265. Includes Callaghan's comments on his career.

Davis, Herbert J. "Morley Callaghan." *The Canadian Forum,* 15 (December 1935), 398-99.

Davis, Robert Gorham. "Carla, Sam and a Dying Pope." *The New York Times Book Review,* October 15, 1961, 4 and 30.

Fajardo, Salvador. "Morley Callaghan's Novels and Short Stories." A doctoral dissertation submitted to the University of Montreal, 1962. A limited but sensitive study.

Fenton, Charles A. *The Apprenticeship of Ernest Hemingway.* New York: Farrar, Straus and Young, 1954.

Lewis, Wyndham. "What Books for Total War." *Saturday Night,* LVIII, 5 (October 10, 1942), 16. A discussion of the stories included in *Now That April's Here.*

McPherson, Hugo. "The Two Worlds of Morley Callaghan: Man's Earthly Quest." *Queen's Quarterly,* LXIV, 3 (Autumn 1957), 350-65.

Moon, Barbara. "The Second Coming of Morley Callaghan." *Maclean's Magazine,* 73 (December 3, 1960), 19 ff.

Perkins, Maxwell. "To Morley Callaghan." *Editor to Author. The Letters of Maxwell E. Perkins.* Edited by John Hall Wheelock. New York: Scribners, 1950, 74-77.

Preston, B. "Toronto's Callaghan." *Saturday Night,* 51 (January 18, 1936), 12.

Scott, Frank R. "Lorne Pierce Medal: Morley Callaghan." *Royal Society of Canada Transactions 3rd Series,* 54 (Proceedings, 1960), 56-57.

Steinhauer, H. "Canadian Writers of Today." *The Canadian Forum,* 12 (February 1932), 177-78.

Watt, Frank W. "Morley Callaghan as Thinker." *Dalhousie Review,* 39 (Autumn 1959), 305-13.

Weaver, Robert L. "A Talk with Morley Callaghan." *The Tamarack Review,* 7 (Spring 1958), 3-29.

Wilson, Edmund. "Morley Callaghan of Toronto." *The New Yorker,* XXXVI, 41 (November 26, 1960), 224 ff.

———. "That Summer in Paris." *The New Yorker,* XXXIX, 1 (February 23, 1963), 139 ff.

———. *O Canada: An American's Notes on Canadian Culture.* New York: Farrar, Straus and Giroux, 1965.

Wilson, Milton. "Literature in English." *The Canadian Annual Review for 1960.* Toronto: University of Toronto Press, 1961.

Woodcock, George. "Lost Eurydice: The Novels of Morley Callaghan." *Canadian Literature,* 21 (Summer 1964), 21-35.

Index

Index